NIGER DELTA OIL: INJUSTICE IN FOCUS

ENE I. UDIOKO (Ph.D)

© ENE I. UDIOKO (PH.D)

All rights reserved. No part of this publication may be reproduced, stored in a retrieval system or transmitted in any form or by any means: mechanical, electronic, photocopying, recording or otherwise, without the prior written consent of the copyright owner.

DEDICATION

I dedicate this book to my Lord and Savior Jesus Christ.

In Him I am able to write this book. I love you Jesus.

PREFACE

The Niger Delta of Nigeria is a boiling cauldron and a Pandora box that has exploded in the past and will likely continue to simmer for many generations until drastic steps are taken by all stakeholders to end the current political, economic and environmental impasse in the country's economic basket. The stakeholders include the host communities, the state (local, state, and federal governments), oil and gas companies and other multinationals active in the Niger Delta, the elite of the Niger Delta, the civil society, and the international community. Nobody doubts that Niger Delta is the real (not proverbial) goose that lays the golden eggs in Nigeria.

Approximately 90 percent of foreign exchange earnings and 80 percent of federal revenues for the last 30 year come from oil, the so called Bonny, sweet, "light" oil.

The Niger Delta is believed to hold at least twenty billion barrels of oil reserves. Nigeria pumps 2 million barrels of oil daily from the Niger Delta. Although Nigeria has earned more than $280 billion dollars over the past 30 years from oil exploration, the environment and living conditions of the oil producing communities is a misery tale of unparalleled proportions. For the inhabitants of the oil producing communities, everyday basic activity is a gargantuan struggle. They cannot drink water because of oil pollution, cannot enjoy gainful employment because their traditional sources of livelihood have been destroyed, cannot hunt because their wildlife is gone, cannot send their children to school or enjoy basic healthcare because of abject poverty, and; cannot enjoy basic transportation, electricity and telephone service because of the "Nigerian" factor.

Nigeria's current political experiment will continue to be hounded by the environmental, health and economic morass of Niger Delta. The Niger Delta issue is a complex web of political betrayal at all levels of government (local, state and federal), endless economic marginalization, and massive environmental insensitivity and neglect. More so, the Niger Delta question is not amenable to quick organizational fixes, amnesty, political expediency, inflammatory rhetoric or double talk. Indeed, Niger Delta represents the rot of Nigeria's polity and its chicanery tendencies and the diabolical machinations of unrepentant elite both from the Niger Delta and the corridors of power in Abuja. The Niger Delta question also transcends the usual Nigerian past time of simplistic ethnic jingoism, atavistic political leadership, cult and personality following, and self-imposed immunity from personal and collective responsibility.

The pertinent question at this juncture is very simple: should Nigerians that occupy the source of our enormous national wealth enjoy an equitable standard of living, pursue economic freedoms with minimal discomfort, and live a healthy life free from avoidable environmental hazards? It is not believed that any Nigerian or multinational conglomerate can argue otherwise or respond in the negative. Consequently, it is rational to ask the following questions: what went wrong in the Niger Delta since 1956? How and when did it go so wrong? Can anything be done to rectify the wrong and assure that it will never happen again? The writer believes that the die is cast for Niger Delta. No present or future government in Nigeria can ever neglect the unjust situation in Niger Delta without major repercussions. Let it be pointed out that the Niger Delta question will not be resolved by rhetoric or grandstanding. This problem will require hard-nosed negotiations, strategies, and resolve. The following chapterisation shall attempt to address the questions posed in this preface as well as other contemporary paradox in the Niger Delta.

Chapter one reviews relevant literature that juxtaposes incidence of poverty as it relates to oil exploration in the Niger Delta region. In chapter two, an analysis of theoretical frameworks of two scholars are undertaken. Here, we explore Humphrey's (2005) six rival families of mechanisms that explains the relationship between natural resources and conflict, as well as Nussbaum's capabilities approach. Chapter three attempts an examination of the origin of oil exploration in Nigeria: the characterization of Nigeria as a rentier state, and a brief background of the Niger Delta region.

In chapter four, effort is made to delve into various constitutional provisions regarding the sharing of revenues in Nigeria and how it metamorphoses to the present paltry thirteen percent derivation allocated to the Niger Delta states. Chapter five focuses on specific critical issues which shape the Niger Delta struggle. How resistance politics started in the region, is the subject matter of chapter six. In chapter seven, dynamics of resistance politics and conflicts are succinctly examined. The various militant groups which emerged for the struggle, are reviewed with detail attention given to the Movement for the Emancipation of the Niger Delta (MEND).

Chapter eight hinges on the plight of the Niger Delta

women, their struggles and protests, against oil multi-nationals and the federal government. At the centre of the causes of the backwardness and exploitation in the Niger Delta, are the oil transnational corporations which extract crude oil from the region, these and some few communities victimized and destroyed in the region for demanding their rights are undertaken in chapter nine of the book.

In chapters ten and eleven, we look into the federal government attempts to address the problem of Niger Delta region with regard to the establishment of some commissions as well as appraisal of the performance of these bodies, with a view to the development of the Niger Delta.

Chapters twelve and thirteen reviews the amnesty programme of the federal government to the "repentant militants" in the Niger Delta, and a post- amnesty programme proposal, is proffered in the section in the form of development model which derives inspirations and working mechanisms from fifteen (15) African Development models attempts (Akinola 2007, 2008, 2010). In chapter fourteen, an analysis of the issue of blood oil in Niger Delta, factors providing enabling environment for oil bunkering or blood oil business to flourish in the region, and the fruitless efforts by the federal government to check mate blood oil business in the Niger Delta, are examined. Issues of corporate social responsibility is the focus of chapter fifteen, in the chapter, we look into attempt by Shell Petroleum to bring succour to the people of Niger Delta in areas of healthcare services, educational initiatives and youth development initiatives. While chapter sixteen explore, the role of federal government and social responsibility in the oil industry as nexus for corporate social development in the Niger Delta.

Chapter seventeen and eighteen juxtaposes solutions as the way forward in resolving the Niger Delta problems.

The roles of the federal government, the Niger Delta states, the transnational oil companies and international community are previewed. The final chapter suggests a scenario obtainable in the United States of America in which oil and gas laws are modeled in favour of the oil producing communities.

Finally, my joy will drive much from the contribution that this book is able to make in removing the mystique around the Niger Delta region, leading to a better understanding of the problem in the region with a view to ensuring lasting peace and development in the oil region in particular, and Nigeria in general. It is my hope that this book will be an asset to all and sundry.

ENE I. UDIOKO

TABLE OF CONTENTS

CHAPTER ELEVEN

The Ministry of Niger Delta Affairs

CHAPTER FOURTEEN

CHAPTER FIFTEEN

CHAPTER SIXTEEN

**Federal Government and Corporate Social Responsibil-
ity
in the Oil Industry: The Possibility of Corporate Social
Development   -   -   -   -
**

ENE UDIOKO

LITERATURE ON THE NIGER DELTA REGION

CHAPTER ONE

REVIEW OF RELATED LITERATURE
ON THE NIGER DELTA REGION

Nigeria is the world's 13th largest oil producer, and the 6th largest in OPEC. In the domestic sector from 1970 to 1999 oil generated almost $231 billion for the Nigerian economy, constituting between 21 and 48 percent of GDP. Nigeria has an estimated oil revenue of 32 billion barrels – sufficient for 37 years at the current rate of production. Oil dominates the Nigerian Economy. Between 2000 and 2004, oil accounted for around 79.5 percent of total government revenues and around 97 percent of foreign exchange revenues. This rise in oil wealth has not translated into significant increase in living standards in Nigeria. In fact, the rise in poverty and inequality coincides with the discovery and export of oil in Nigeria. As Sala Martin and Subramanian (2003) show, in 1965, when oil revenue was about US $33 per capita, GDP per capita, was $245. In 2000, when oil revenues were $325 per capita, GDP per capita was stalled at the 1965 level. Evidence such as this has led to widespread acceptance that

Nigeria has suffered from the resource course and according to Sala Martin and Subramanian (2003); Waste and poor institutional quality stemming from oil has been primarily responsible for Nigeria" poor long-run economic performance.

The oil boom in Nigeria has been driven by oil extracted from the Niger-Delta. Oil wealth, from the Niger Delta Region, is largely responsible for sustaining the Nigerian Federation. Despite fuelling much of Nigeria's economic growth, the Niger Delta is somewhat marginalized from Nigeria's national development. Essentially, there is a significant disconnection between the wealth the region generates for the Nigeria Federation and the transnational oil companies extracting oil from the region, and the region's human development progress. Analysis of poverty and human development indicates paints a dismal picture for the Niger Delta. Poverty incidence increased in the Niger Delta between 1980 and 2004 as shown in Table 1 below:

Table 1: Incidence of Poverty in the Niger-Delta Region – 1980 – 2004

Country/States	1980	1985	1992	1996	2004
Nigeria	28.1	46.3	42.7	65.6	54.4
Edo/Delta	19.8	52.4	33.9	56.1	Delta 45.35
					Edo 33.09
Cross River	10.2	41.9	45.5	66.9	41.61

Imo/Abia	14.4	33.1	49.9	56.2	Imo 27.39
					Abia 22.27
Ondo	24.9	47.3	46.6	71.6	42.15
Rivers/Bayelsa	7.2	44.4	43.4	44.3	Rivers 29.09 Bayelsa 19.98

Source: *National Bureau of Statistics*

The region's human development index (HDI) is 0.564 and while this is slightly higher than the Nigerian HDI of 0.448, the area rates are below regions or countries with similar gas or oil reserves (e.g. Venezuela is 0.772 and Indonesia is 0.697). When further disaggregated to the local government level, the Niger Delta Human Development Report shows that state and regional HDI scores Mark inequalities in human development among oil producing communities. Significantly, local government areas without oil facilities appear to have fewer poor people than those with oil facilities. The report also concludes that decline in the HDI has been steeper for the Niger Delta states than the rest of Nigeria. In addition, the high earnings of some oil industry workers leads to localized price distortions, driving up prices and so constraining the purchasing power of ordinary people and making it difficult for many to meet the costs of basic needs such as: housing, healthcare, transportation, education and thus making poverty more pervasive than conventional measures reveal.

LITERATURE ON THE NIGER DELTA REGION

Comparatively, poverty and inequality in Nigeria has strong regional concentrations, resulting in significant levels of regional disparity. Table 2 below shows that poverty is considerably higher in the Northern part than the Southern part of Nigeria:

Table 2: Trends in Poverty levels by zones in Nigeria (1980-2004)

Zone	1980	1985	1992	1996	2004
South –south	13.2	45.7	40.8.	58.2	35.1
South-East	12.9	30.4	41.0	53.5	26.7
South-West	13.4	38.6	43.1	60.9	43.0
North-Central	32.2	50.8	46.0	64.7	67.0
North-East	35.6	54.9	54.0	70.1	72.2
North-West	37.7	52.1	36.5	77.5	71.2

Source: *National Bureau of Statistics*

It is germane to state that the poverty of the Northern part of Nigeria is more in terms of human development index (HDI) than infrastructural development index (IDI). On the other hand, the Niger Delta Region has better developed human capital through individual self-effort, but has been infrastructural neglected, and marginalized by the federal government of Nigeria. The poverty of the North as recognized by the colonial masters led to the amalgamation of the Northern and Southern Protectorates in 1914, as the Surpluses from the

South was used to net-off the deficit from the northern part of the country after the amalgamation. Regrettably, the poverty level of the North has consistently dragged back and prevented the South from developing, especially the Niger Delta Region, from where the major source of revenue to the federation is derived.

LITERATURE ON THE NIGER DELTA REGION

The Niger Delta Region today is a place of frustrated expectations and deep-rooted mistrust. Unprecedented restiveness at times erupts in violence. Long years of neglect and conflict have fostered a siege mentality especially among youths who feel they are condemned to a future without hope and see conflict as a strategy to escape deprivation. While turmoil in the delta has many sources and motivations, the preeminent underlying cause is the historical failure of governance at all levels. Declining economic performance leading to rising unemployment or underemployment, the lack of access to basic necessities of life like water, food, shelter and clothing, discriminatory policies that deny access to positions of authority and prevent people from participating in shaping the rules that govern their lives – these all indicate that governance overtime has fallen short of the people's expectations.

Many reports have chronicled the region's monumental problems. The magnitude of the problems the people of the Niger Delta is best illustrated in the report by the World Bank in 1995. In 1995 the two volumes study entitled: "Defining an Environmental Development Strategy for the Niger Delta" was conducted by the Industry and Energy Operations Division of West Central Africa Department of the World Bank.

The region is described in the following words:

> The Niger Delta has been blessed with an abundance of physical and human resources, including the majority of Nigerian's oil and gas deposits, good agriculture land, extensive forests, excellent fisheries, as well as a well developed industrial base, a strong banking system, a large labour force, and a vibrant private sector. However, the region's unfulfilled and its future is threatened by deteriorating economic conditions that are not being address by present policies and actions.

LITERATURE ON THE NIGER DELTA REGION

The report goes further to lament that:

> ... Despite its vast reserve, the region remains poor (GNP) per capita is below national average of $280.

The report continued:

Education levels are below the national average and are particularly low for women. While 76 percent of Nigerian children attend primary schools, this level drops to 30 percent in some parts of the Niger Delta. The Poverty level in the Niger Delta is exacerbated by the high cost of living. In the urban areas of Rivers state, the cost of living index is the highest in Nigeria.

The next chapter shall attempt to explore two theoretical approaches to explain the issue of resource, conflicts and a failure of basic justice as they relates to the Niger Delta.

ENE UDIOKO

THEORETICAL EXPLANATIONS

CHAPTER TWO

THEORETICAL EXPLANATIONS

2.1 The Synergy between Resources and Conflicts

There is a correlation between oil and conflict that suggests causation. Although scholars have always tried to use the three major counter-examples of Botswana, Namibia and South Africa as Mineral-dependent African countries that do not suffer from this symptom (Mokhawa, 2005:21; Paes, 2005:305-23; Omeje, 2008) and a few other big success stories of rich oil-producing countries like Norway, The United Arab Emirates and the Sultanate of Brunei, does not mean that the thesis is wrong or can be ignored.

Thus, there are several theories about how oil fuels conflicts that emerged out of large-number of quantitative studies that found strong correlations between oil dependency and various kinds of violence. Humphreys (2005) outlined six rival families of mechanisms that could explain the relationship between natural resources and conflicts: (a)

The greedy rebels mechanism; (b) The greedy outsiders mechanism; (c) The grievance mechanism; (d) The feasibility mechanism; (e) The weak states mechanism; and (f) The sparse networks mechanism.

In the greedy rebel's mechanism, the booty character of natural resources motivates rebels to take up arms and / or continue fighting. This mechanism has three variants. In the first variants, domestic groups may engage in quasi-criminal activities to benefit from resources independent of the state as exemplified by piracy, oil bunkering and kidnappings going on in the Niger Delta region. In the second variant, natural resources increase the prize value of capturing the state. This means that either variant could lead to either situation taking place-weakening the state in order to make its capture possible. The third variant states that if natural resources are concentrated in a particular region of the country, it makes for the possibility of that region thinking it could secede from the rest of the country, and that it would be possible to withstand the pressure and become prosperous.

THEORETICAL EXPLANATIONS

In the greedy outsiders' mechanism, greedy outsiders might be ready to intervene militarily – either directly or through support for internal conflicting factions in order to gain or maintain control over lucrative resources. The existence of natural resources may be an incentive for third parties – state and corporations – to engage in or indeed foster civil conflicts, as seen and proved in the Niger Delta with the involvement of Shell B P in the Ogoni Crisis, for which they have paid huge sums as compensation to the people.

In the grievance mechanism, perceived deprivation of producing regions and social groups create grievances and trigger violent uprising, especially secessionism in producing regions. Natural resource dependence can be associated with grievance rather than greed. This is because countries that depend on resources may experience transitory inequity as part of the developing process; such economies may be vulnerable to terms of trade shocks, that is, they may likely be dependent on a small number of commodities for their export earnings; the process of extraction may produce grievances, either through forced migration or as a result of environmental damage or loss of land rights; or natural resource wealth may be seen to be unjustly distributed as seen in the case of Niger Delta.

In the feasibility mechanism, natural resources provide the means for rebel finance. Natural resources could provide a way to finance rebellions that have been started for other reasons, thereby increasing the prospects of success: this can be done either through control of production during the conflict or by raising revenues in advance to gain control of the resources "booty futures" (Ross,

2002).

THEORETICAL EXPLANATIONS

In the weak states mechanism, resource abundance reduces the quality of state institutions, and makes internal violent conflict more likely. State structures may be weaker in natural-resource-dependent economies, and this argument focuses on the strength of the linkage between the state and society. This argument means that when citizens are not taxed by government, they have less power over them as they would have less information about government activity, weaker incentives to monitor government behaviour, and fewer instruments at their disposal to withdraw support from governments. Accordingly, resource-dependent states may have little compulsion to respond to the demand of their citizens or crate structures that engage their citizens (Collier and Hoeffler, 2005:512). Conversely, governments that rely on natural resources rather than on taxation have weakened incentives to create bureaucratic institutions. That is, such states are likely to have weak structures because they gave less need for intrusive bureaucracies to raise revenue; and as such, the domestic economy is divorced from the state.

In the sparse networks mechanism, rentier economies have a one-sided integration in the world economy and hence cannot develop thick terms of exchange conducive for peace and stability. The importance of natural resources may lie in their impacts on the daily economic activities of the citizens of an economy and how these in turn affect attitudes of citizens or relations between citizens. Thus, natural-resource-dependent economies may have weak manufacturing sectors and corresponding low levels of internal trade. This is because it is given that trade is associated with relationship and cohesiveness among people. No one fights his trading partners as wherever there is commerce, manners are gentle. Moreover, through trade, partners understand one another's cultures and this helps in reducing the risks of conflicts between them.

Given the above theoretical explanations to buttress the fact that there is a synergetic linkage between resources and violence or conflict, this book hypothesizes that the Niger Delta conflict and underdevelopment is a consequence of the Nigerian state's inability to have a coherent resource wealth governance policy. This premise shall further be consolidated by employing the Capabilities Approach by Martha Nussbaum.

THEORETICAL EXPLANATIONS

2.2   Martha Nussbaum's Capabilities Approach

The Capabilities Approach: Difference between Sen's and Nussbaum's:

Capabilities Approach is a normative theory proposed by Martha Nussbaum. The theory was pioneered by the Nobel winner, economist Amortya Sen in Development Economist. According to Nussbaum, Sen uses the concept "to indicate a space within which comparisons of quality of life (or as he sometimes says, standard of living) are mostly fruitfully made. Instead of asking about people's satisfactions, or how much in the ways of resources they are able to command, we ask instead, about what they are actually able to do or to be". Contrary to Sen's version, Nussbaum noted that her goal in her own version of the capabilities approach is to go beyond the merely comparative use of the capability space to articulate an account of how capabilities, together with the idea of a Threshold level of Capabilities, can provide a basis for central constitutional principles that citizens have a right to demand from their government". Thus the difference can be structured in the following ways;

First, Nussbaum notes that her own version of capabilities theory is partial theory of justice because its concern is only the account of minimum core social entitlements and as such, the notion of threshold plays more important role in her version of capabilities theory than the notion of full capability equality. Her theory does not say anything about how justice would treat inequalities above the threshold. The threshold of capabilities which is important for her will serve as a practical and realizable policy guide for policy makers. Consequently, she intends to make it "real and con-crete rather than abstract". This distinguishes it from Sen's full Capabilities theory and as Nussbaum wrote, Sen nowhere uses the idea of a threshold.

Second, both versions of Capabilities theory asserted some form of equality as a necessary in-gredient in achieving well being of human person. Nussbaum claimed that her version of Capabilities approach is philosophically grounded in Marxian/ Aristotelian ideas of human dignity and flourishing. Unlike hers, Sen's version of capabilities Approach lacks this grounding but only made reference to them in his work. Thus she writes "nor has Sen ever attempted to ground the Capabilities Approach in Marxian/ Aristotelian idea of truly human func-tioning".

THEORETICAL EXPLANATIONS

Third, while Sen did not provide list which can serve as a political and social framework, Nussbaum's versions of the approach did through her list of the the Cen-tral Human Capabilities which she sees "as basis for a specifically politically conception and a spe-cifically politically overlapping consensus. Having presented the differences in the two versions of Capabilities Approach, the next section of the book shall delve into details so as to unveil why Nuss-baum's version accounts for a development para-digm that is fully human.

2.3 The Idea of Human Person in Nussbaum's Capabilities Approach

Martha Nussbaum who's Capabilities Approach, is feminist based especially as it pertains Third World women, personally lived with Indian women in March 1997 and December 1998 in her bid to write a real and concrete work. She writes in her book that "women in much of the world lack support for fundamental functions of a human life. They are less well nourished than men, less healthy, more vulnerable to physical violence and sexual abuse. Nussbaum observed that in many nations of the world, women are not full equals under the law: they do not have the same rights to make a contract, the same rights of association, mobility and religious liberty". Nussbaum observes as well that women themselves are burdened with what she called 'double day' because of duo responsibilities of a tasking employment outside their homes on the one hand and the domestic responsibility of house work and child care on the other hand. For her, this inhibits the opportunities for play and for the cultivation of their imaginative and cognitive faculties. Thus she argues that all these unequal social and political circumstances give women unequal human capabilities. She went further to argue that the capabilities approach should be able to provide for people in general and third world women in particular who have not lived lives they truly value simply because they are women, real opportunities to lived those lives. In explaining the approach, Nussbaum presents two-fold intuitive ideas as a foundation for a capabilities approach. She writes;

THEORETICAL EXPLANATIONS

The intuitive idea behind the approach is two-fold; that certain functions are particularly central in human life, in the sense that their presence or absence typically understood to be a mark of the presence or absence of human life and second, this is what Marx found in Aristotle – that there is something that is to do with these functions in a truly human way, not merely an animal way.

The first part of the intuitive idea deals with what makes "the good life" which is connected to the concept of human flourishing. According to Aristotle, the question of 'good' is all about what it means to flourish, which for him is connected to notion of living well as the ultimate end of human life. That is why he said that the ultimate end of human life is eudaimonia which he described as the state of living well. Commenting on the Aristotelian idea, Nussbaum writes,

To the Greeks, eudaimonia means something like 'living a good life for a human being'; or as a recent writer John Cooper

has suggested, human flourishing. 'Aristotle tells us that it is equivalent to living well and doing well.

Explaining further on the above observation, Nussbaum wrote that " we believe that human life is worth living only if a good life can be secured by effort, and if the relevant sort of effort lies within the capabilities of most people. This idea is apropos to Aristotle's who writes in his Nicomachean Ethics that "it is evident that eudaimonia stands in need of good things from outside: for it is impossible or difficult to do fine things without resources". Resources are necessary ingredients for the attainment of this end (eudaimonia) though not ends in themselves. Good life is able to do and able to be, which is actualized through the availability of resources.

THEORETICAL EXPLANATIONS

The second part is on a life lived in a dignified way and hence deals with human dignity. On this she wrote "we judge, frequently enough, that a life has been so improvised that it is not worthy of the dignity of the human being, that is a life which one goes on living, but more or less like an animal, unable to develop and realize one's human power". Making this philosophical conception of human power, Nussbaum makes connection to Karl Marx whose theory on labour emphasized that human person is an end in itself and as such should not be treated as merely "Means to an End". Marx who took his stand by departing from Kant in some important respects (stressed along with Aristotle) that the major power of human being need material support and cannot be what they are without it. He however noted that his Aristotelian heritage is shaped by the Kantian notion of inviolability and dignity of the person. Capturing this Marxist stand, she wrote that "the core idea is that of human being as a dignified free individual who shapes his or her own life in cooperation and reciprocity with others, rather than being passively shaped or pushed around by the world in the manner of a flock or animal". A life that is really human is one that is shaped through by these human powers of practical reason and sociability.

In summary, Nussbaum asserts that "Capabilities Approach makes each person a bearer of value and end". Nussbaum while quoting Marx holds that, it is profoundly wrong to subordinate the ends of some individuals to those of others. That is the core of what exploitation is, to treat a person as a mere object for the use of others. Thus she argues that, "what this approach is after is a society in which persons are treated as ends each worthy of regard, and in which each has been put in a position to live really humanly". Nussbaum however, rephrased Marx's principle of each person as end, articulating it as a principle of each person's capability: the Capabilities sought are sought for each and every person, not, in the first instance, for groups or families or states or other corporate bodies though she argued that may be important for the realization of capabilities.

THEORETICAL EXPLANATIONS

2.4   The Ten Central Human Capabilities

In contrast to and in the bid to address the criticism of Sen's Capabilities Approach which did not identify any capabilities list in deference to pluralistic society, Nussbaum identifies a set of basic capabilities. Her reason for the list is to provide a philosophical underpinning for an account of basic constitutional principles that should be respected and implemented by the governments of all nations, as a bare minimum of what respect for human dignity requires. She argues that the list isolates those human capabilities that can be convincingly argued to be a central importance in any human life in whatever else one pursues or chooses. And for her the central capabilities "are not just instrumental to further pursuits; they have value in themselves, in making the life that includes them fully human. They are held to have particularly pervasive and central role in everything else people plan and do. She notes that though the list serves as a guide for policy makers and governments, she however stated that it is open-ended and subject to revisions as it suits a particular society especially with attention to their histories.

Below is Nussbaum's list of ten central human

capabilities which ensures full human dignity if each and every one of the features in the list is satisfied.

They are as follows;

1. Life: Being able to live to end of a human life of normal length and not dying prematurely.
2. Bodily Health: Being able to have good health which includes reproductive health, adequate nourishment and shelter.
3. Bodily Integrity: Being able to have physical security with rights over one's body.
4. Senses, Imagination and thought: Being able to use the senses to imagine, think and reason and to do things in a 'truly human' a way informed and cultivated by an adequate education.
5. Emotion: Being able to have attachments to things and people outside ourselves.
   THEORETICAL EXPLANATIONS
6. Practical reason: Being able to form a conception of the good and engage in critical reflection about the planning of one's life.
7. Affiliation: (a) Being able to live with others and sympathize with them. (b)

Having the social basis of self-respect and non-humiliation. Not to be discriminated on the basis of sex, race, religion, caste, ethnicity or national origin.

8. Other Species: Being able to live with concern for and in relation to the natural world.
9. Play: Being able to laugh, play and enjoy recreations.
10. Control Over One's Environment: (a) Being able to participate in political process that govern one's life. (b) Being able to own property and seek employment on equal basis.

Nussbaum however, emphasized that the list is a list of separate components. She argues that "we cannot satisfy the need of one of them by giving a larger amount of another one. All are central importance and all are distinct in quality". At the same time, the items on ;the list are related to one another in many complex ways. For example, if one has all the principles but he is always in constant fear of being killed due to insecurity, then his well-being is compromised. Therefore, Nussbaum argues that any lack in one of these, no matter what else he or she has will be lacking in humanness.

2.5   Critique of Nussbaum's Approach

Most critics of Nussbaum's Capabilities Approach direct their criticism not on the threshold of capabilities since people are unarguably entitled to a set of basic capabilities. Rather, criticisms are directed to her list of capabilities. First, according to critics, Nussbaum capabilities list fails to account for certain exception as a result of complexity of human life and culture. On this, Des Gasper asks, "Why make a list of universal capabilities?" According to Gasper, Nussbaum's setting of the criteria assumes that "a deep thinking individual could rationally determine what is rationally binding in a situation". What this means is that Nussbaum seems to arbitrarily prescribe what is good for people irrespective of culture and time. Gasper's criticism concerns procedure because Nussbaum's Capabilities list is one party arbitrary prescription of what is good life without the participation of the sectors who are stakeholders in the issue. Thus he argues that such procedure 'overrides' the individual preference and rights to construct the meaning of their life as they see fit".

THEORETICAL EXPLANATIONS

Nussbaum however argues that the list is the starting point of a universal concept of what it really means to be human and the making of the list is to make it concrete. According to her, the list is not 'Exhaustive account of political justice", there may be other important political values, closely connected with justice, that it does not include". Thus she noted that it is an 'open-ended and subject to ongoing revision and rethinking, in the way that any society's account of its most fundamental entitlements is always subject to supplementation (or deletion). To make it more inclusive which will include not only the policy makers but the stakeholders in issue, Alkire, suggested participatory procedure. Alkire writes that participation plays a constructive role in clarifying value and value priorities. For her, "participation refers to the process of discussion, information gathering, conflict and eventual decision making, implementation and evaluation by the groups directly affected by the activity".

Nussbaum acknowledged the importance of participation when she writes that, "the items on the list ought to be specified in a somewhat abstract and general way, precisely in order to leave room for the activities of specifying and deliberating by the citizens and their legislatures and courts". Though Alkire spelt out the detail of the participatory procedure, Nussbaum however, acknowledged participation as a necessary ingredient for the realization of the theory of the society. Through participation, the people affected by the issues will make decisions that affect them, there by empowering them.

The second criticism is non-contradiction of no-prioritization of the capabilities list. According to Philip McReynolds, Nussbaum writes that the capabilities list represents an authentic moral pluralism and each component in the list is an independent good or value in the sense that each is independently worthy of pursuit and none of the components is subordinate to the others or to any overarching single ends. McReynolds argued that in Nussbaum's list, two capabilities – practical reasons and affiliation – stand out from the rest of the list. Nussbaum acknowledged this when she writes "Among the capabilities, two practical reason and affiliation – stand out as of special importance since they both organize and suffice all the others, making their pursuit truly human".

THEORETICAL EXPLANATIONS

The essence of Nussbaum's list is to promote the need to take people's actual aspirations seriously since it entails human rights. On this Nussbaum writes, "the fact the human beings desire something does count, it counts because we thinks that politics, rightly understood, comes from people and what matters to them, not from heavenly norms". Even though many of the criticisms on Nussbaum's Capabilities approach hover around capabilities list, but there are more to Nussbaum's Philosophy than her list. And as David Crocker write that Nussbaum's list should be seen not as condition, but as relevant criteria. The list does not set a standard for human decency, rather it indicates the basic criteria that must be met and the need for social and political institutions who are duty bound to promote the list. Doing so will address urgent and real issue of human development and backwardness especially, in Niger Delta.

Therefore, the overriding importance of this approach is that, it understands that needs, particularly basic needs unlike interest cannot be traded, suppressed, or bargained for, thus any attempt to do this, leads to conflict. According to Aristotle, as quoted in Ikejiaku, social strife and revolutions are not brought out by the conspirational or malignant nature of man; rather revolutions are derived from poverty and distributive injustice. Hence, when the poor are in the majority and have no prospect of ameliorating their condition, they are bound to be restless and restitution through violence. No government can hold stability and peace when it is created on a sea of poverty and injustice. The level of poverty in the Niger-Delta region has gone beyond the level of absolute poverty to the level of poverty, a term coined by Ikejiaku to describe the practical absolute poverty where the majority find life excruciating because it is difficult to meet or satisfy their basic need. It is pathetic that an average Niger Deltan has grown poorer over the past decades, notwithstanding the enormous natural resources available in the region.

ENE UDIOKO

CHAPTER THREE

HISTORY OF OIL IN NIGERIA

The Second World War terminated the initial search for oil in Nigeria by Shell D'Arcy Explorations parties, an Anglo-Dutch consortium, who was grant of a sole concession over the whole country, in 1937. This search however resumed in 1946, after the war, In 1953, Shell-BP started commercial production and exportation of oil in Oloibiri, at the rate of 5,000 barrels per day. This production rate soon doubled within the next one year. With the sole concession policy abandoned and exclusive exploration rights introduced to encourage companies of other nationalities in line with a policy of accelerating the pace of exploration. In 1961, Mobil Gulf (now Chevron), Agip, Safrap (now Total final ELF), Tenneco and Amoseas (now Texaco) join in the search for oil, both onshore and offshore, with considerable success.

One noticeable fact is that most of the oil companies listed above and those still operating in Nigeria are from both Britain and United States of

America. This is in no way a mere coincidence. The issue as captured by Jean Marie Chevalier (1980) is that, "The history of the oil industry is the history of imperialism". The dominant position of Britain in the balance of power equation of the world in the early part of the last century assured her hegemonic position in the global configuration of power after the second world war, a situation that threw up America as the new centre of imperialism, Britain was relegated next to the United States.

This international character of the oil companies as we shall see later, is part of the problematic of the sustainable development in the Niger Delta in particular and Nigeria in general. However, the balance of power between the Nigerian state and the local communities where these oil conglomerates are located is such that favor the oil companies. Both the mineral oil ordinance and the Petroleum Profit Tax Ordinance, both in 1959, were highly skewed in favor of the oil companies.

HISTORY OF OIL IN NIGERIA

Oil occupies an important place and, plays a pivotal role in the Nigerian Political economy. According to Obi (1997), oil accounts for 95% of export earning and over 80% of national revenue. The growth of oil revenue greatly influenced the activities of the Nigerian State. The public sector expenditure for instance, increased significantly. The government was able to invest a large amount of revenue in building social and economic infrastructure. According to a World Bank Country report (1990), "the expenditure of the Federal Government doubled between 1973 and 1974 and doubled again between 1974 and 1975". Oil enable the Nigerian State to persecute the thirty months Nigerian civil war without any form of external borrowings. There is a sense in which it could be argued that the issue of who controls the nation's oil resources was part of the underlying factors, which ignited the Nigerian civil war.

The operation of oil business in Nigeria involved both private and public actors. While the private actors are mainly foreign oil multinationals, with some pockets of local oil marketers and intermediate actors, the public sector actors are various agencies of state, such as the Nigerian National Petroleum Corporation (NNPC), Department of Petroleum Resources (DPR), etc. This however, is not to suggest that the dichotomy between the private and public sectors is forever held in a water tight compartment. Starting form 1971, the Nigerian state entered into a collaborative business alliance with foreign capital in the oil sector. It however, acquired equity holding in both ELF and AGIP, which as at 1974, was as high as fifty-five percent.

The linkage between oil and the Nigerian State has often led to the characterization of Nigeria as a rentier state. This is so because with the discovery of oil, the traditional agricultural and mineral exports like cocoa, palm oil, groundnut, cotton, tin, coal, etc, that hitherto supplied the nation's foreign exchange and contributed to larger percentage of her Gross National Products (GNP) were relegated. The consequence of this is streamlining the percentages of people that are involved in the production of the national wealth. With oil, only a very small proportion of the nation's population is directly involved in the production of the nation's wealth. And with the technology for oil exploration and exploitation totally in the hands of foreigners, the Nigerian State and its citizens are primarily reduced to commissioned agents.

HISTORY OF OIL IN NIGERIA

This incidence of non-productive national revenue base evidenced the growth of authoritarianism, political alienation of the people, corruption, environmental degradation and conspicuous consumption to the disadvantages of national development. The authoritarian tactics of the state in Nigeria in general and the Niger Delta in particular, can be understood in this context. The next section of this book shall look at the characteristics of the Nigerian State.

3.1   A Review of Nigerian State

The Nigerian State insertion into the global capitalist system was a deliberate act of Western imperialism to have the country as one of its peripheral social formations for the procurement of slaves in the first instance and, later raw materials and cheap labor for the development of western capitalism. When trade became the dominant concern of the relationship between Nigeria and its imperialist lords, it was an unequal one. Following the scramble and partition of Africa in Berlin in 1883 amongst European powers, to consolidate its hold on her imperial colony, the British colonial authorities formally took-over direct political control of Nigeria at the break of the twentieth century. The combine effects of its trading policies, political tendencies and educational and socialization processes, promoted the development of a class of local elite with the same organic interest with those of the colonizers. The totality of colonial experience in Nigeria was a veritable case of exploitation, brutalization and injustice. The colonial state was in essence one that was anti-people, anti-development and irresponsible. The power of the colonial state in Nigeria, as elsewhere was not only absolute but arbitrary (Ake: 2001:2).

HISTORY OF OIL IN NIGERIA

While capitalism, despite its numerous limitations was a system with the potential to increase production; though the majority of the producers are alienated from their products, colonial capitalism was a different ball game. Contrary to limited state participation, which normally informs the logic of capitalism, the variant institutionalized in Nigeria involved a robust state participation. Primacy was given to trading and commercial activities instead of production and manufacturing, with the centrality of foreign capital to the economic existence of the country firmly and irrevocably established. This ensured the entrepreneurial class needed for capitalist growth were never develop, hence the state acted as a platform for primitive capitalist accumulation. The point being underscore is that the multi-dimensional issues of corruption, authoritarianism, development of underdevelopment and over-centralization of power in the hands of the federal government has its historic root in the politics of the colonial period in Nigeria.

It was against this background that the writer agrees with Williams (1980:11) assertion that, "Nigeria suffered, not only from the development of Capitalism, but also from the backwardness of development". The long-run implications of this process, which impacted greatly on post-colonial politics in the country, is the inability of the country to assume the development of her citizens despite her enormous human and material resources. The struggle for independence in Nigeria for many reasons was a colossal failure. The nationalist agitations in Nigeria had two major objectives; one, at the initial stage, it was to seek a minimal accommodation for the local elite in the functioning and benefits of the spoils of colonial rule. Second, was to ensure the direct control of the exploitative state apparatus already institutionalized by colonial autocracy. It was therefore, not surprising that ideological issues, agenda for development and more importantly, a program for the transformation of the obnoxious colonial state structure never formed part of the demands during the nationalist agitations.

For all intent and purpose, the Nigerian independence struggle; if at all we can call it a struggle, was seriously speaking, a bread and butter business. It would therefore have been surprising to have a progressive consensus agenda for the transformation of the country by the nationalists. It was so bad that the colonial power were in most cases, the mediator in the cutthroat struggle between the so-called comrades in the struggles for Nigeria's independence.

HISTORY OF OIL IN NIGERIA

At independence in 1960, the non-transformation of the colonial state that was inherited ensured the continuation of colonialism in the grip of neo-colonialism, with the economy and its ruling class operates totally dependent on western imperialism. Expectedly, liberal capitalism was the informing ideology for development. Consequently, from the very beginning, the masses were alienated from the leadership. Given their inability to mobilize the masses for development; in fact, they deliberately demobilized and repressed the masses; the problem of development and its sustenance assumed serious dimensions. The net effect of ideological bankruptcy, visionless leadership, elite conspiracy with imperialism, state alienation from the people and lack of automatization combine to engender underdevelopment, poverty, squalor, unemployment diseases, maladministration, corruption, and other social malaise.

What come out of the foregoing is that the Nigerian ruling class is not only dependent; it is parasitic and very corrupt, lacking any meaningful material base for the perpetuation of its privileged control, the instrumentalities of the state comes in handy as a tool of primitive accumulation. And as we shall see presently, with the dominant position assumed by oil in the political economy of Nigeria, the multinational corporations in control of the technologies for exploitation of oil from the Niger Delta on behalf of the state and its decadent class becomes untouchable, while the just desire of the people of the Niger Delta in particular and Nigeria in general, for quality existence continue to be treated with contempt, making authoritarianism a preferred formula of governance in place of democracy. And when democratic pretence becomes inevitable, disrobes it of any meaningful content.

HISTORY OF OIL IN NIGERIA

3.2   **Niger Delta: Back-**

ground

The Niger Delta is one of the largest deltas in the world, probably the third largest on earth. The region is regarded as one of the nine most difficult deltas of the world comparable to the Mekong, the Amazon and the Ganges. It is situated in the central part of southern Nigeria. It lies within latitudes 4-degrees north to 6-degrees north, and longitudes 5-degrees east to 8-degrees east. The Niger Delta is a geographical landmark that grew out of the fanning of the River Niger into thousands of square kilometers of swamps, waterways, vast flood plains, Mangrove forest areas, and fishing villages.

Geographically, the western limit is the Benin River while the Cross River is the limit on the east. It is triangular in shape having its apex some twenty kilometers north of Ndoni in Rivers State. It covers an area of about 70,000 square kilometers, and is spread across nine of the thirty-six states of Nigeria. These include Bayelsa, Delta, Rivers, Edo, Akwa Ibom, Cross River, Ondo, Abia, and Imo states. It is endowed with immense natural resources, particularly crude oil. The process of the formation of the present delta started about 75,000 years ago and over the centuries, accumulation of sedimentary deposits washed down the Rivers Niger, and Benue. The present coastal formation consists of a chain of barrier islands interspersed by river estuaries, giving the delta a shape like a bird's foot. The population of the Niger Delta is about 12 million people, and is growing at 3% a year. There are more than 20 ethnic groups in the area with links to the linguistic groups of Ijaw, Edo, Igbo, Delta Cross, Efik, Ibibio, Annang, Ogoni and Yoruba. The Ijaws are the largest groups, and probably moved to the Delta over 7,000 years ago.

According to the 1998 Niger Delta Environmental Survey, oil production and other industrial activities, population growth, agriculture, logging and fishing, are just some of the factors that have greatly impacted on the evolution of the Niger Delta.

However, public attention has tended to focus on the appropriation of oil from the region. From the discovery of the first commercially viable oil wells in Oloibiri in 1956, to the present day, the issue of oil production and its effect on the environment has been the source of constant friction between oil companies and the host communities. According to the Shell Petroleum Development Company, most environmental problems related to the oil industry are due to oil spills, gas flaring, dredging of canals and land taken for construction of facilities. These oil-related activities have affected agricultural and fishing activities in the host communities, the major economic preoccupation in these areas. Large oil spills, depending on their location, may go undetected for many days or even months with untold damage to the fragile ecology of the Niger Delta. Thus, the simple desire of Niger Delta oil producing communities to survive according to their age-old symbiotic relationship with the environment, has collided with the Federal Government/Petro-business desire to extract oil, with minimum fuss and disturbance.

HISTORY OF OIL IN NIGERIA

In the next chapter, we shall look into the history of constitutional provisions that directly or covertly impacted negatively on the people of Niger Delta region.

GENESIS OF POVERTY AND DEPRIVATION IN THE NIGER DELTA

61

CHAPTER FOUR

GENESIS OF POVERTY AND DEPRIVATION IN THE NIGER DELTA

4.1 Pre-Independence Constitution

As already pointed out, the geographical entity known as Nigeria, came into being with the amalgamation of the Northern and Southern Protectorates in 1914. However, it was not until 1951 that an acceptable constitutional frame-work was worked out by the colonialist and people of Nigeria. The 1951 constitution introduced fundamental changes into the relationship between the colonialist and the natives on the one hand and between the native Nigerian groups themselves, on the other. The constitution was promulgated after an unprecedented process of consultation with the people of Nigeria as a whole. The consultation was total from the villages to a national conference. The outcome of the consultations marked the first formal introduction of federalism into Nigeria. The conference noted that: we have no doubt at all that the process already given constitutional sanction, and fully justifies by experience, of devolution of authority from centre to the regions should be carried much further so that a federal system of government can be developed.

The general conference was of the opinion that over centralization would be a grave mistake "in this vast country with its widely differing conditions and needs". It meant that when given the opportunity to decide what political arrangement, that would suit living together, the federal system was the popular choice of Nigerians. Federalism is an arrangement whereby powers are shared between a federal and central authority and a number of component units in such a way that each unit, including the central authority exists as a government separately and independently from the others, operating directly on persons and property within its territorial area, with a will of its own and its own apparatus for the conduct of affairs and with an authority in some matters exclusive of all others. In a federation, each government enjoys autonomy, a separate existence and independence of control of any other government. Each level of government exists, not as an appendage of another government, but as an autonomous entity in the sense of being able to exercise its own will in the conduct of its affairs free from directives from any other government. It was expected that federalism would help in the effective management of heterogeneity, enhance democratic consolidation and facilitate socio-political and economic co-existence, while at the same time creating unique divergences, which would subsequently facilitate the process of nation building as well as development.

4.2 The Independence and Post-Independence Constitutions of the 1960

The 1960 independence and 1963 republican constitution of Nigeria epitomized some elements of a true federal system. The 1950 National conference had been followed by other consultations in 1953, 1954, 1957 and 1959, in which the practice of federalism was perfected. An important feature of these constitutions was the extensive powers granted the regions, making them effectively autonomous entities and a revenue arrangement, which ensured that the Regions had the resources to carry out the immense constitutions, the true federal system was made of strong regions and a central government with limited powers; certain features emphasized the thoroughness of the federal system in this period, these included:

(a)   Each Region had its own separate constitution, in addition to the federal constitution.

(b)   Each Region had its own separate coat of Arms and Motto different from that of the federal government.

(c)   Separate Judicial system for each Region which enabled the Regions to have not only High courts, but also Regional court of Appeal.

(d)   Revenue Allocation system under these constitutions was based on derivation.

The federal constitution of 1960 in Part 2 of chapter 9 allocated the country's revenue to the two levels of government and shared other federal collected revenue between them, section 140 of the 1963 constitution made provision for the sharing of the proceeds of minerals, including mineral oil, it states that:

There shall be paid by the federal government to region, a sum equal to fifty percent of proceeds of any royalty received by the Federation in respect of any minerals extracted in that region and any mining rents derived by the federal government from within any region.

Interestingly, each region strove to have a dominant revenue-yielding product, the North had groundnut and cotton, the West had cocoa and rubber, and the East had oil palm. Thus, the federal principal at this point was a basis for defining competition between the groups for social and economic progress of Nigeria. It was discovered that, the East and the Northern Region matched any move by the western Region towards industrialization and vice versa. It was a period in which the competition among the various Regions of the federation generated economic gains that ushered in industrialization, and massive investment in education. This progress was made not because of natural resources, but because of the competitiveness which caused the leaders in the 1960's to become creative and rigorous in public choice making. There was a steady progress, especially between 1956 and 1966, before the military intervened in politics, and crude oil assumed the position of the largest single foreign exchange earner.

GENESIS OF POVERTY AND DEPRIVATION IN THE NIGER DELTA

4.3   Centralization of Revenue Source

As noted earlier, at independence in 1960, Nigeria was a federation of three powerful regions. Each regions was provided a tax base composed largely of revenues easily identifiable as originating from these regions. A pooling account was also established for sharing revenues considered to be of national significance such as mining rents and royalties and custom duties, import and export – excise duties and company taxes. The principle of derivation played an important role in the sharing of pooled resources at this time because the country was concerned with setting the right incentives for tapping local revenue resources and encouraging fiscal responsibility in the regions.

The first misguided, but direct attack on federalism in Nigeria was by the military in January 1966, when General Aguiyi Ironsi overthrew the democratic government and promulgated Decree No. 33 and 34 of May 1966, abolishing the federal system and replacing it with a unitary form of government. Because of the general inclination of Nigerians for a federal system of government, the abolition was resisted and repulsion for Aguiyi Ironsi's unification of the country by military first led to violent and bloody riots in the North, which culminated in a second military coup in July 1966, then a reversion to the federal system and later a civil war. The abrupt and unexpected termination of democratic rule by the military initiated a process that steadily eroded the powers of the Regions (later states) with the transfer of several items hitherto in the residual and concurrent lists to the exclusive list.

However, the first major development that made the dominant political elite at this time to rethink its role in the control of the oil industry was the Nigerian civil war. While the control over oil cannot be said to be at the heart of civil war, the contest of the right to revenue payments between the federal government and the government of the secessionist Biafra brought to the fore the need for a closer control of the industry by the dominant ruling elite. Also, given the atmosphere of the civil war, the ruling elite saw the concentration of powers at the centre as a strategy for strengthening the political class and building some platform for cohesion.

GENESIS OF POVERTY AND DEPRIVATION IN THE NIGER DELTA

In 1967, the military introduced a twelve state structure to replace the existing four regions and through a series of decrees issued form 1969, set about the process of centralizing fiscal powers, with exclusive powers to legislate on solid/mineral oil and natural gas, "these decree completely undermined and subverted the federal basis of association", especially the Petroleum Act of 1969 and the Land Use Act of 1978. In 1970, the Federal government allocated the bulk of federally collected revenue to the central government. It also jettisoned the principle of derivation (for need) and a lump sum transferred to cover the fixed cost of running a government, in state allocation. It also introduced a dichotomy between onshore and offshore mining and assigned offshore rents and royalties to itself. The channeling of all distributable revenues through a pool account in 1975 expanded the scope of revenues collected by the federal government and shared by the various governments.

The process of centralization was completed with introduction in 1980 of the Federation Account (FA) to hold all federally collected revenues, including the 20 percent onshore mining rents and royalties hitherto conceded on the basis of derivation, and inclusion of local governments in the federation account revenue sharing arrangements. The principle of derivation was now given only a token recognition by the introduction of a special fund for mineral producing areas to receive a small transfer of between one and one point five percent (1.5%) from the federation account and to be shared by states on the basis of derivation. The Federal government, which had become unitary in practically every sense of the word, relied on 'periodic grants' or special allocations to the States. The arrangement did not change significantly during the brief civilian administration of 1979 to 1983 and the second military period of 1983 to 1999. In order to find avenue for expending the increased resources at its disposal as a result of this centralization of revenue, the Federal government began to extend its activities to areas of expenditure once reserved for states, first by the process of encroachment and later by formal legislations-backed take over. The federal government became directly involved in primary and basic education, agriculture, banking, industry and commerce etc. Some of these involvements were later formalized in the 1979 and 1999 constitutions.

GENESIS OF POVERTY AND DEPRIVATION IN THE NIGER DELTA

**4.4   Conse-
quences of Centralization**

A few questions are however pertinent at this juncture. They are:

(i)   What happened to the resources, which the

governments of the former four regions – depended upon to fund their respective economic and infrastructure development programs before the advent of oil?

(ii)   What happened to the groundnut pyramids, the cotton, the plywood, the rubber, the timber, the cocoa and the palm oil / kernel?

Economic indices show that the per capita income and overall standard of living of Nigerians were higher in the era of regionalism and fiscal federalism. The perennial haggling over revenue allocation is indicative of how the country has deviated from the original idea of federalism, which was adopted by the founding fathers of the nation. They would never have imagined that the federation of their dream would give rise to states that cannot survive without handouts from the Federal Government. It is disheartening therefore to note that an overwhelming majority of the states can hardly survive without the constant support of the Federal Government. Rather than develop locally based resources, most of the states now wait for largesse form the Federal Government, in the name of allocation from oil revenue.

Over centralization of power has stifled local initiative. Instead, it has promoted inefficiency and fostered a sense of over dependence on the federal government. In fact, it has created a situation, a system or mechanism that discourages work by having 'booty' which is shared every month. If people are not working but depend on booty sharing, there cannot be increased economic activity. You cannot nurture a people on a system of booty sharing without production and expect development. This paternalistic form of federalism, which is the order of the day in Nigeria, cannot be sustained, especially with the increasing crisis and conflicts in the Niger Delta region.

GENESIS OF POVERTY AND DEPRIVATION IN THE NIGER DELTA

4.5   Effect Of Centralization on the Niger Delta Region

Beginning from 1969, the politics of Nigeria, whether military or civil became that of determining the control of oil resources. As Saro-Wiwa aptly observes, "oil is not only money, it has been at the centre of Nigerian Federalism, for a long time, with the federal government reserving for itself, "a huge chunk of oil revenue". However, the nature of rent-based income that occurred from oil production and the neo-colonial ruling elite has elicited a pattern of development that is excessively distorted. One area in which the underlying crisis in the economy has been felt most in recent times is the Niger Delta, the main crude oil producing region. Today, only thirteen percent of rents and royalties from oil exploration is now allocated on the basis of derivation, meaning far less resources to the Niger Delta, despite the degradation and underdevelopment associated with oil production in the region. The Federal Government controls the rents and royalties, allocates it and decides policies on investment, technology, the environment, and employment. At the peak of the false oil boom in the economy, the oil producing regions were subjected to abject neglect. As earlier stressed, the oil producing areas remain most under-developed areas of the country, lacking in modern infrastructures, such as roads, education, medical facilities, electricity and so on. Further effects of centralization on the Niger Delta are highlighted in chapter five of the book under ten critical issues in the Niger Delta struggle.

NIGER DELTA OIL: INJUSTICE IN FOCUS

CRITICAL ISSUES IN THE NIGER DELTA STRUGGLE

CHAPTER FIVE
CRITICAL ISSUES IN THE NIGER DELTA STRUGGLE

Having undertaken a purview and background on Niger Delta, let us briefly examine some critical issues that have shaped the Niger Delta struggle. These issues represent direct and indirect correlates of the violence and repression in the Niger Delta. The writer also believes that identifying the critical issues will provide a pathway to an eventual long lasting solution to the Niger Delta question. These however does not represent my way-forward to the problems of Niger Delta which shall be discussed in the later part of this book. The following ten critical issues are identified and discussed below:

1) Oil Spillage
2) Gas flaring
3) Environmental degradation
4) Poor Health Status
5) Poverty
6) Pipeline explosions
7) Limited government / public sector

presence
8)   Distrust of the government / petrobusiness alliance.
9)   Lack of basic infrastructure
10)   Political Marginalization

5.1   **Oil Spillage**

The issue of oil spillage is as old as drilling itself, in every area where there is oil exploration, oil crude spills on the surface of the earth and surrounding waters. This kills plants, defertilizes the earth, harms animals, fowls, farm lands, and destroys aquatic life. Consequently, farming and fishing industries, the major sources of economic sustenance in oil producing areas have suffered irredeemably from oil exploration. The delicate ecosystem of the Niger Delta, oil spills destroy natural freshwater reservoirs that serve as sources of drinking water, with potential health hazards. Since oil and gas pipelines criss-crosses the Niger Delta, it is sometimes difficult to spot spills immediately and take remedial action. However, the most difficult aspect of oil spillage is the recurring battle between oil/gas companies and host communities over the role of 'sabotage'. In Nigeria, oil/gas companies by law are not obligated to pay compensation for spills from deliberate, destructive acts. Rows over who will clean up oil spills, and pay compensations are often at the core of acrimonious relationships between host communities and oil/ gas companies.

However, one thing is very clear: oil spillage is a fact of life in the oil producing communities with widespread pollution of creeks, rivers, farmlands, and mangrove forests.

5.2 Gas Flaring

Nigeria flares more gas than any other nation in the world. At least 75% of Nigeria's total gas production is flared, and about 95% of associated gas, a by-product of crude oil extraction from reservoirs. According to the Nigeria's Department of Petroleum Resources (DPR), between 1998 and 1999, the total volume of gas utilization for industrial and domestic use in Nigeria was approximately 916 million standard cubic meters. However, during the same period, the oil producing companies flared about 1.7 billion standard cubic meters of associated gas. Much of the flared gas is methane, with high warming potentials, and potential destructive health hazards. Although Nigeria since 1969 had laws requiring oil-producing companies to utilize the associated gas from their exploration activities, not much has happened in this area. Gas flaring has continued unabated. For the host communities, gas flaring is a cause of acid rains that corrode metal roofing sheets atop houses, increase soil temperatures, and visibly damage vegetation near the flares. However, there is an ongoing scientific controversy over the link between gas flares and acid rain according to conclusions by independent consultants, the World Bank, and other multinationals. The Shell Petroleum Development Company contends that the low sulfur-dioxide content and nitrous oxide in the gas flares are unlikely to lead to acid rains. Nevertheless, for the inhabitants of the host community, the acid rain is real with adverse effects on their lives. The Federal government recently 'ordered' the oil/gas companies to end gas flaring on or before 2010.But 2010 has come and gone, yet there is no end to gas flaring.

CRITICAL ISSUES IN THE NIGER DELTA STRUGGLE

5.3   Environmental Degradation

According to the world Bank, there are five great plagues of mankind: war, famine, pestilence, environment pollution, and death. The Niger Delta is in the throes of becoming an environmental waste-basket. Form the oil spills to the round-the-clock gas flares and effluents from industrial waste; the fragile ecosystem of the Niger Delta is under constant assault. However, it is still a mystery that no comprehensive study of oil exploration in Niger Delta and its effect on the environment exists. The role of population growth, industrialization, and physical development are also important environmental research issues. The Niger Delta Environmental Surveys, largely funded by the oil/gas industry appears to be tentative, formative steps of the survey and the unsettled issue of intellectual and scientific independence, the jury is still out on the long term effectiveness and veracity of its eventual findings. It is safe to say that until the rumblings of the Ogoni people, the issue of environmental degradation was not a central political or economic issue in Nigeria. Although Nigeria has an impressive array of environmental laws, it is no secret that enforcement has been lax. Apart from the concern for their staff safety, oil companies have been largely clay-footed regarding the safety hazards of oil exploration in host communities. For example, in the oil producing Obagi town of Rivers State, the road that leads into the village is literally the lifeline of the community. The noise of gas flare and industrial machinery makes it impossible for pedestrians to hear the sound of oncoming traffic. Also, the digging of burrow pits constitutes danger to the lives of the people. Many individuals have drowned in these pits. Many have fallen into the pits and sustained serious injuries that led, in some cases, to their death. Burrow pits still abound.

5.4 Poor Health Status

From a simple perspective, the scarcity of clean drinking water in the water soaked Niger Delta is not only an irony but also a potential health hazard. According to the landmark 1999 Human Rights Watch Report on Niger Delta, an oil producing community reported that 180 people died following a large scale oil spill; spills had made people sick or hospitalized, and; fish from contaminated streams, sometimes tastes of kerosene (paraffin) suggesting hydrocarbon contamination. It is important to note that the long term effect of hydrocarbons on humans is still evolving, with speculations on carcinogenic consequences. Recently, the mangrove forest conservation society of Nigeria (MFCSN) filed a lawsuit in Port-Harcourt High Court accusing the Nigeria Liquefied Natural Gas Company (NLNG) of complicity in the high rate of AIDS in the Bonny community of River State. Various fact finding missions to the Niger Delta have documented complaints of increasing ill health among inhabitants of oil producing areas, and shortened life spans. It is however surprising that the comprehensive health status of Niger Delta inhabitants is not available.

5.5   **Poverty**

The destruction of the land and water ways of the Niger Delta region has denied the people their major sources of fishing and farming livelihoods. One of the most visible images of Niger Delta is the distinct world that exists: The affluent government / petro business alliance versus the wretched poverty of host communities. The economic strangulation of some oil producing communities is total, with unemployment rates of 80 percent or more. Families in these communities find it difficult to keep their children in school because of limited disposable income. Consequently, intergenerational poverty has become a fact of life in these communities. Access to healthcare is also sporadic, as families have to make gut-wrenching choices between hunger and clinical care. Poverty and the attendant struggle for scarce resources remains a fact of life in Niger Delta.

5.6 Pipeline Explosions

Niger Delta is criss-crossed by approximately 10,000 miles of pipelines. Most of the pipelines were laid more than 30 years ago. Contact between water and steel will eventually result in rust, wear, tear, and leakage of highly inflammable liquids. Since 1999, there have been a series of pipeline explosions, with hundreds of people roasted alive. In most cases, villages are accused of siphoning oil from pipelines. The central question should be: what will cause a rational human being to risk his or her life for a bucket of gasoline? Perhaps, faced with severe and sustained economic hardship, the pangs of hunger may outweigh the risk of death.

5.7 Lack of Sustained Government Presence

The oil producing communities lack any meaningful government presence. In most of these communities, any evidence of local, state or federal government presence exists in the fertile imaginations of government spin-doctors and sycophants.

However, there is a recurring government presence in Niger Delta: police stations and military patrol units armed to the teeth and ready for 'action'. For the inhabitants of the oil producing communities that sustains the Nigerian state, basic necessities such as functional schools and hospitals are luxury items. If they dare agitate for these luxuries, the state will 'show' them for disturbing the peace.

5.8   Lack of Basic Infrastructures

Lack of basic infrastructure in the Niger Delta is perhaps one of the most visible signs of neglect. Electricity, drinkable water, roads, elementary and secondary schools, health centres, and telecommunication system are 'not present' in Niger Delta. At the beginning of the present political experiment in May 1999, the oil producing state of Bayelsa was not connected to the national electricity grid. Oil companies have active community based projects that are promoted with evangelical fervor in media establishments. However, these projects are fewer than expected by oil producing communities, limited in scope, and sometimes, patronizing. The oil companies appear to have become experts on 'tokenites', where token gestures are exaggerated with expectations of veneration. The state (local, state, federal) appears to have become experts on 'earmarks' of major projects without any evident 'eye mark' of completed projects. The lack of basic infrastructure in Niger Delta is not only outrageous but also wicked.

5.9 Distrust of Government and Oil Companies

In developed countries, the most strategic and resilient partnership is the military/industrial complex. However, to survive the military/ industrial complex in developed countries must remain sensitive to the final arbiters of public policy: Citizens that vote in democratic elections. In Nigeria, the dominant superstructure is the government/ petro business alliance that acts with impunity. Every Nigerian government, including the present government, brooks no opposition to this unique alliance. This powerful alliance with mutual benefits will do anything humanly possible to prosper. The oil producing communities understand the existence and importance of the alliance, and consequently recognize the state and oil/gas industry as one and the same. Thus, it is an exercise in futility for the oil/gas industry to distinguish their obligations to host communities from that of the state.

5.10 Political Marginalization of the People

The inhabitants of Niger Delta have always agitated for fairer treatment in Nigeria. The Willinks Commission was set up by the then colonial governor, Sir James W. Robertson in 1959 in response to the Niger Delta question. The findings of this commission eventually led to the establishment of the Niger Delta Development Board. The Mandate of this Board was to focus on the peculiar developmental needs of Niger Delta. From the establishment of the Niger Delta Basin Development Authority in 1978, lack of robust funding remained a major drawback. Very little could be achieved in the face of daunting ecological, infrastructural and developmental needs of the Niger Delta. The OMPADEC and the Niger Delta Development Commission (NDDC) as well as the ministry for Niger Delta are the recent attempts by the Federal Government to respond to the Niger Delta question. Successive leaders of the Niger Delta have accused the Nigerian polity of political and economic marginalization. The feeling of marginalization is also pervasive that some Niger Delta scholars believe that the non-inclusion of the Niger Delta in Nigeria's National Flag is a strong signal of state-sanctioned policy of neglect. The state has responded by creating state and local governments, appointing elite from oil producing areas to top government positions, and rewarding selected indigenes with lucrative contracts and government largesse. The oil/gas industry also responded with juicy contracts to selected elite from oil producing areas, providing basic infrastructure to select communities, and hiring / promoting sons and daughters of oil producing areas to key positions in the industry. However, like all short-term political settlement, the bondage simply covers the festering sores, leaving the source of the problem. The vast majority of the inhabitants of oil producing areas have either benefited from the government programs nor enjoyed sustained 'philanthropy' from the petro business. Surprisingly, the managers and strategists of this powerful and wealthy government / petro busuness alliance failed to recognize or acknowledge the absence of the natural third rail of the alliance: The oil producing communities. For the past 45 years, the government/petro business alliance has ignored its inevitable partner, the oil producing communities, with increasingly unacceptable costs and consequences. The struggle to end the political marginalization of Niger Delta will continue until the recognition and inclusion of oil producing communities as the third rail of the government / petro business alliance.

CRITICAL ISSUES IN THE NIGER DELTA STRUGGLE

HISTORY OF RESISTANCE POLITICS IN THE NIGER DELTA

CHAPTER SIX

HISTORY OF RESISTANCE POLITICS
IN THE NIGER DELTA

The Niger Delta has a long history of resistance politics, dating back to the eighteenth and nineteenth centuries, when the region opposed the early attempts of European traders, to gain access to the interior where goods traded on the Atlantic coast were sourced. By the late nineteenth century, resistance by some local potentates was finally overcome by the British, setting the stage for the colonization of Nigeria. The British divided Nigeria into three regions corresponding with the major ethnic groups (Hausa-Fulani in the North, Yoruba in the west, and Igbo in the East), thus setting the stage for ethnic cleavages and politics, including the agitation of ethnic minorities against perceived ethnic majority domination. Nigeria's independence in 1960 only changed the character of the struggle for self-determination. This time the ethnic groups of the Niger Delta region, who were minorities in two of the three regions of a federation dominated by three numerically larger ethnic groups, sought to have autonomous regions of their own to prevent their continued marginalization and neglect by the larger groups.

The earliest violent attempt after independence to forceful assert regional autonomy over the Niger Delta took place in February 1966, when an ethnic minority Ijaw militant, Isaac Adaka Boko, led the Niger Delta Volunteer Force (NDVF) in an abortive attempt to secede from Nigeria and establish a Niger Delta Republic. At stake then, as now, was self-determination and the ownership and control of the oil in the region (Boro 1982, 119-120), which Boro and his supporters feared would be seized by Eastern region government, dominated by the Igbo ethnic majority, and the new 'Unitarist' Nigerian military government, let by General J. T. U. Aguiyi Ironsi, an Igbo officer (Obi 2001,21).Initially sentenced to death after being found guilty of treason by a court, Boro and his followers were freed, after another military coup led by military officers of Northern origin resulted in Ironsi's overthrow and death, and his replacement with Colonel Yakubu Gowon as the new head of state. Within a year, the federal military government under General Gowon created 12 states in 1967, of which three –Rivers, mid-west, and south-east – were in the Niger Delta. By this time, oil, largely found in, and produced form the Niger Delta, had become a significant factor in Nigerian politics.

Upon his release, Boro joined the Nigerian Army and fought in the civil war on the federal side to defend the interests of the ethnic minorities of the Niger Delta form perceived Igbo domination and prevent the oil fields of the region from falling into the hands of the rebel Biafran (Igbo) forces (Boro 1982). Boro died at the war front shortly before the Nigerian civil war ended in 1970. His bravery and exploits in furthering the cause of Ijaw freedom made him a hero in the eyes of the people, and his legacy was to be revived in the 1990s by Niger Delta Militants Struggling for local autonomy and resource control.

Several developments after the civil war ended in 1970, had implications for the struggle of the Niger Delta ethnic minorities. These included the increased transfer and centralization of the control of oil revenues from the regions to the federal military government, and the vast expansion in local oil production and its impact on the fragile Niger Delta environment. This provided some justification for renewed agitation by the ethnic minorities that felt that the federal military government had short-changed them: they supported it during the civil war, only to lose access to a considerable proportion of the oil produced from their region. Rather than having a right to 50% of oil revenues on the basis of the derivation principle of revenue allocation, their share was progressively reduced until it dropped to a mere 3% in the early 1980s. Various ethnic minority groups such as the Ijaw, Ogoni, Urhobo, Isoko, Ilaje, Egi, Ikwere, and Itsekiri had began to remobilized using peaceful methods to protest against the activities of oil companies and neglect by the government. These took the form of petitions, reports, and articles in local newspapers. Pressure groups also emerged to demand for creation of new states in the region and greater representation in federal institutions. The expansion of the oil industry, the economic crisis following the fall in world oil prices in the early 1980s, and the adverse socio-economic effects of economic reform policies contributed to worsening conditions in the Niger Delta. These in turn contributed to the intensification of the struggles in the Delta.

HISTORY OF RESISTANCE POLITICS IN THE NIGER DELTA

6.1 Dimensions of Conflict in the Niger Delta

Conflicts in the Niger Delta are three dimensional processes which are centred on social identity, resource control and development in the area. The first process is that any conflict is centre on social identity in as much as it opposes ethnic groups, where crude-oil is exploited, to the Federal Government of Nigeria (the unquestionable right owner of the crude-oil wealth). The second process is the agitation for resource control by different ethnic groups, especially, those living where oil is exploited, while the third process is the inter and intra communal conflicts between communities over land and water spoiled by crude oil deposit. This was further highlighted by Eteng that:

> *The oil economy created an environmental crisis and consequently disorganized socio-economically the peasant communities in which oil was found. The expectation of this commodity alimented established endowment and ownership exchange entitlement system and processes without offering the people adequate employment opportunity (1998:49).*

In some case, some of these changes led to agitation for resource control and bloody conflicts in the Niger Delta. According to Suberu (1996), the difficulties and deprivations of the oil producing communities in the Niger Delta have invariably brought them into direct confrontation with not only the oil prospecting companies in the area but even government agencies.

Against this backdrop, Alameiyesigha (2005), had argued that the external economic interests in the Eastern Niger Delta between 1854 to date led to negative consequences like the displacement of people and underdevelopment of the region, which invariably aggravated existing antagonisms, hostilities and conflicts over the natural resources in the area. Put differently, Uroh (1998:9), argues that external intervention opened a new phase of conflicts in terms of reorganization of the cultural values of the people to suit the economic interest of the external (western) powers. At this point, it is relevant to state that the analysis of the external influence on the conflicts in the Niger Delta is included because intra and inter communal conflict, social identity and resource control agitations began to be noticed between 1900 and shortly after independence in 1960, reaching its climax in the mid 1990s.

HISTORY OF RESISTANCE POLITICS IN THE NIGER DELTA

In view of the implications to the people's survival and development, any attempt to exploit its resources and distort it cultural values would, under normal circumstances, be challenged and in most cases lead to violent conflicts. Thus, conflicts in the Niger Delta region have continued to degenerate. The agitation for resource control, intra-inter communal conflicts with the strivings of others have remained a defining characteristics of the region. According to Lenin:

> *It is only a study of the sum of the strivings of all the members of a given society or group of societies that can lead to a scientific definition of the result of conflicts in the society (1984 :250).*

Similarly, the study of the nature of conflicts in the Niger Delta is also advanced in Akukue's argument that:

> *Since 1900 when the first conflict ensued in the Krani-Legbara as a result of the introduction of the obnoxious offensive and unacceptable illegal collection of taxes, and the forceful acquisition of private lands, it leaves a question mark on the people's survival and development of its resources (2003: 103).*

Moreover, unrestrained exploitation of the environmental resources is done at the expenses of the oil producing communities in the Niger Delta, which do not benefit enough from the oil revenue (Adetula, 1996). As a result, the people agitate for the control of natural resources in the area, including crude oil mining.

HISTORY OF RESISTANCE POLITICS IN THE NIGER DELTA

One important element of conflicts in the area is that attachment to development. Development in this regard means the people's ability to maintain their cultural values and sustain their traditional economic resources. Development is expected to improve and advance the condition and standard of living of the people. But development in the Niger Delta is elusive; according to Ibeanu (1997: 24), the persistence of violence distorts and destroys resource flows, thereby threaten development and the people's livelihood. Therefore, efforts are directed toward agitation to control resources like crude oil, the "black gold" – that is being exploited for external interests. Weighed against the background of the immense resources, the nation generates from the area, the Niger Delta region could be said to be relatively underdeveloped especially when compared to places like Lagos, Abuja, Kano and Kaduna, which without oil are yet developed. Apart from references to conflict and agitation to control resources as obstacles to development in the Niger Delta, there is also identity agitations by the various ethnic groups who want to break-off from the Nigerian Federation. As Bassey (2003: 22) observes, the unique combination of these features, like ethnic identity agitation, constitute the spectrum of conflicts in the Niger Delta.

As already pointed out before, the people in the Niger Delta believe that they are undeveloped economically and socially despite the enormous revenue made from oil in their areas. This view highlights the undercurrent of conflicts, social identity and resource control agitations that are being propagated by MEND and MOSOP. Table 3 reveals the historical nature and reasons for the struggle. According to Douglas:

> *Our struggle is militant without being Military. The majority of Nigerians do not want to address the Niger Delta problem. So we must struggle for our rights, our struggle is for democracy. It is for true federation; to control what is ours, to control our resources (1999: 66).*

Table 3: Historical Perspectives of Social Identity Conflicts and Resource Control Agitation in the Niger Delta

S/N	Associations	Nature of Conflict	Year	Social Identity	Demand	Fear of the People	Requirements
1.	Izon youths Urohobo youths Itsekiri youths	Youth revolt against stop of middle Benin, the core Delta	1886	Ijaw Urohobo Itsekiri	Restoration of middle men by the colonial authorities	Displacement of livelihood	Commitment and determination for fairness and justice
2.	Isaac Adaka Boro's Revolt	Declaration of Niger Delta Republic	1966	Izon Ijaw	Self-determination and control of resources in the Niger Delta	Economic and political marginalization-underdevelop-ment	Courage, bravery, determination to achieve equity and fairness for the people
3.	MOSOP	• Declaration of Ogoni nation and Ogoni Bill of Rights. • Ogoni versus Shell war • Ogoni versus FG agencies: Polic and army	1990 1993 1997	Ogoni	Self-determination, control of resources in Ogoni land, creation of Ogoni state and more Local government areas	Oil exploitation, under-development, political and economic marginalization, language extinction.	Courage, determination, consistence, focus, and goal oriented struggle for justice, fairness and equity.
4.	MEND	• Ijaw youth versus oil companies • Urhobo youths versus Oil companies • Itsekiri Youths versus oil companies • Chikoko youths versus oil companies • Isoko youths versus oil companies • Egi clan youths versus oil companies • Ikwere youths versus oil companies • Delta youths policy statement: Kaiania Declaration	1998 To 2008	Ijaw Urhobo Itsekiri Chikoko Isoko Egi	Self-determina-tion, Niger Delta Republic, Resource control, Political relevance, Security of life and property	Underdevelopment, language extinction, resource exploitation, environmental degradation, political and economic marginalization	Purposeful commitment, goal oriented struggle, consistence, emancipation, dignity and respect for the people

Source: *Fieldwork, Madubuike 2009*

It is evident in the above table that injustice, exploitation of resources and gross underdevelopment of the area, have been the main causes of conflicts. Understandably, in view of these predicaments, the people and especially the adults and the youths took the initiative of constituting militias to fights for their collective existence and survival. As a result, the government, during the military regime, took power away from local communities in critical areas meant to ensure their sustainable development (Jamuno, 1999: 22). This approach by the government in the past until now has sustained the conflicts in the Niger Delta despite amnesty program initiated by Late President Yar'Adua. This situation further excites the fears of the people that they are being marginalized and exploited by the ruling groups (the three major ethnic groups: Igbo, Yoruba and Hausa).

Another fundamental point which propels conflicts and agitations in the Niger Delta lies in the fact that the principles of derivation in revenue allocation between 1953 and 1995 are inconsistent and so are the Land Use Decree of 1978, 1993, the Petroleum Pipeline Decrees of 1969 and 1991, and the National inland waterways Authority Decree No.13 of 1997. Through this undemocratic governance, the Niger-Delta region was systematically disempowered, underdeveloped and socio-economically marginalized. Chronologically, table 4 below shows systematic patterns of reduction in the principles of derivative revenue allocation between 1953 and 1995.

HISTORY OF RESISTANCE POLITICS IN THE NIGER DELTA

Table 4: Systematic patterns of Reduction in the Principles of Derivative Revenue Allocation:

Major Revenue Derivative	Year	Allocation (Percentage)	Ethnic Group/State	Effects
Palm oil and Palm Kernel	1953 to 1960	100% 50%	Igbo	Development, at 50% Unserious protests
Cocoa	1953 to 1960	100% 50%		Development, at 50% Unserious protests
Groundnut and cotton	1953 to 1960	100% 50%	Hausa	Development, Satisfied
Rubber	1953 to 1960	100% 50%	Mid-western	Development, at 50% unserious protests

Crude oil	1970	45%	Rivers state, South Eastern state Mid-western state	Protest, complaints of injustice and marginalization
Crude oil	1975 to 1982	20%	Rivers state Cross River state Mid-western Imo state	Complaints of injustice, fear of under-development, marginalization, fear of political irrelevance, Ethnic identity negotiation
Crude oil	1982 to 1984	2%	Rivers State Imo State Cross River State Delta State Akwa Ibom State	Resource control Agitation, ethnic identity negotiation, marginalization, Underdevelopment, intra-inter communal conflicts.
Crude oil	1984 to 1992	15%	Rivers state Delta state Imo State Cross River State Akwa Ibom State	Intra–inter communal conflicts resource control agitations, ethnic identity negotiation, underdevelopment.
Crude oil	1992 to 1995	3%	Bayelsa state Rivers state, Imo state Cross River State Akwa Ibom State Abia State	Agitation for resource control, injustice, ethnic identity negotiation, conflicts both intra-inter communal, military/police harassments.
	1995	13%	Abia, Bayelsa, Delta, Rivers, Akwa Ibom Cross River State, Imo states	Underdevelopment, political marginalization agitation for resource control, conflicts both intra-inter communal, military/police harassments.

Source: *Fieldwork, Madubuike 2009*

The possible interpretation of the above table is the systematic patterns of reduction in the principles of derivative revenue allocation between 1953 and 1995 reveals the main causes of agitations for resource control and identity in the Niger Delta. For instance, when other resources like palm-oil, Kernel, cocoa, groundnut and rubber constituted the bulk of the national revenue, the allocation formula were based on 100% and 50% but as soon as crude oil became the main source of national revenue, the formula changed unfavorably to the areas from where it was derived. This change in the derivative allocation principle affected development in the areas. As a result, the people reacted through protests and agitations for resource control.

ENE UDIOKO

DYNAMIC OF RESISTANCE POLITICS AND CONFLICT

CHAPTER SEVEN
DYNAMIC OF RESISTANCE POLITICS AND CONFLICT

The Militarization of oil extraction has percolated throughout Niger Delta society, contributing to the shift from non-violent to violent resistance. Resistance has been largely framed in the rhetoric of 'resource control', hinted in the preceding chapter. But the campaign is not entirely free of certain ambiguities and contradictions. It is important to note Gramsci's argument on the 'ambiguity of resistance' (Mittleman and Chin 2005: 17-27), in seeking to fully understand the calculations of expediency and fluid dynamics that underpin the formation, divisions, and shifting positions of the various actors: ethnic minority organizations, militias, and elite factions within the Niger Delta resistance coalition.

Although rooted in the oil-rich Niger Delta, resistance is by no means limited to the region. It spans other levels, national and global, in what can be termed a "geographical rescaling", with various actors and flows interacting in a complex tangle. Depending on the specificities of each moment, or calculations of expediency, they seek to block the process of oil-based accumulation. The strategies deployed also include mobilizing ethnic minority/communal organizations or militias outside of mainstream political parties and pressure groups, using local tradition/ histories and global media to popularize local causes, which are often hinged on repossessing the control of oil. It is important to note that the composition of the resistance 'coalition' is neither homogenous nor fixed. It is constantly evolving, with ethnic minority militia opposed to the state-oil alliance entering into expedient partnerships with Niger Delta ruling elite that is perceived to be the main beneficiary of the wanton exploitation of the region.

DYNAMIC OF RESISTANCE POLITICS AND CONFLICT

The basic assumption that flows through the resistance discourse is that oil extraction is synonymous with dispossession, marginalization, and injustice. This can be gleaned from the Ogoni Bill of Rights, from the Movement for the Survival of Ogoni people (MOSOP), and the Kijama Declaration of the Ijaw Youth Council (IYC). These are charters of demand by Ogoni and Ijaw ethnic minority groups of the Niger Delta who seek to reclaim control and ownership of their natural resources for their own development. It is also writ large in the current campaign and demands of the movement for the Emancipation of the Niger Delta (MEND) – the most recent and insurgent face of Ijaw pan-Delta resistance (Obi 2008, 423-428; Ukiwo 2007), to be discussed in the following section.

MOSOP moved its struggle to the next phase in the 1990s after its demands for "political autonomy", including "the right to the control and use of a fair proportion of Ogoni economic resources for Ogoni development" as articulated in the Ogoni Bill of Rights, was ignored by the federal government. MOSOP linked up with transnational right advocacy networks such as, Human-Rights Watch, Rainforests Action Group, Amnesty International, Sierra club, and Friends of the Earth to globalize its local resistance and increase its pressure on the government and on Shell, the largest onshore Multinational oil Operator in the Niger Delta. It demanded a stop to the environmental degradation of Ogoni land, then payment of oil royalties, compensation for damage already done, and respect for the rights of the Ogoni people. Mosop's spokesperson showed how Ogoni's resources were being tapped by the state-oil alliance, pointing also to the pollution and degradation of the environment as threatening the existence of the Ogoni.

The MOSOP campaign against shell became well known and effective locally and internationally before its "revolution" was literally beheaded in November 1995 by the federal Military government. Although the fate that befell Mosop's leaders, nine of whom were hanged, was to send a signal to other ethnic minority groups that the government would no brook any challenge to its control of oil, Ijaw youth took up the struggle from 1997 onwards. In December 1998, the Ijaw youth council was formed at a meeting of Ijaw activists and representatives from 40 Ijaw clans from across the coastal states of Southern Nigeria. It issued the Kaiama Declaration (KD), which insisted that "we cease to recognize all undemocratic decrees that rob our people / communities of the right to ownership and control of our lives and resources which were enacted without our participation and consent" and demanded the 'Ijaw control of Ijaw Oil'.

DYNAMIC OF RESISTANCE POLITICS AND CONFLICT

Like MOSOP, the IYC appealed to the youth and ordinary people by drawing upon Ijaw traditional beliefs about justice and resistance. This included the use of Egbesu, an Ijaw god or deity of war, whose real significance lay deep in cosmology as a symbol of spiritual protection, conferring invincibility from bullets or other forms of harm, for the Ijaw when they were fighting a 'just war' for liberation. Egbesu initiation rites by Ijaw traditional priests were believed to embolden Ijaw youth intent on joining the resistance militia. In late December 1998, the IYC mobilized the Ijaw through operation climate change, a program of non-violent protest demanding that oil companies leave the Niger Delta before the end of the year. Rather than negotiate with IYC or respond to the demands made in the KD, the military government sent in troops backed by warships that forcefully put down the protests in January, 1999.

When Nigeria returned to democratic rule in May 1999, expectations were initially high in the Niger Delta that this would lead to the demilitarization of the region, reduce tensions, and bring "democracy dividends" to the people. At the same time, the Niger Delta faction of the ruling elite had made the rounds in an attempt to co-opt the leadership of the various social movements and the ethnic and communal organizations, with a view to deradicalizing and demorilizing them or using them for narrow or personal political purposes. After the 1999 election, government security forces remained in the Niger Delta. When a criminal gang operating from Odi, an oil producing community in Bayelsa State, killed some police officers, the town was invaded by the Nigerian army, ostensibly to apprehend the criminals. This punitive expedition resulted in the razing of the entire community and left thousands injured, homeless, or dead. Although the abduction of police officers in Odi was an isolated event, it did not stop military forces from raiding other communities in the Niger Delta such as Olugbobiri, Liama and Gbarantoru (Human Rights watch 2002).

DYNAMIC OF RESISTANCE POLITICS AND CONFLICT

The militarization of the region dialectically led into violent resistance by reinforcing the view that the oppressors would neither listen to the people's demands nor respect their rights. Apart from the perceived 'failure' of peaceful protest to effect a change in the attitude of the state-oil alliance toward the Niger Delta, violent mobilization within and between local communities, alongside elite factionalization, became a source of empowerment for many youth. They adopted violence in navigating the complex terrain of survival in the region, pressuring the local elite and resisting the predatory instincts of the state-oil alliance and its local criminal gangs in the region (Coventry cathedral 2009, 109-131), a development that partly led to the blurring of the boundaries between violent criminality and resistance.

The current dynamics suggest a considerable difficulty in differentiating the upsurge in criminality from that in violent resistance. Ikelegbe (2008), identifies three types of militias in the Niger Delta insurgent, deviant insurgent, and criminal armed groups. The insurgents are described as the fighting arms of ethnic minority mobilization against the state-oil alliance. Examples include the Federal Niger Delta Ijaw Communities (FNDIC), the movement for the survival of Ijaw Ethnic minorities in the Niger Delta (MOSIEND), the Niger Delta Peoples

Volunteer Force (NDPVF), and MEND, all affiliated to the Ijaw/Niger Delta Resource Control Project. Insurgent deviant groups either evolve into insurgent militia or break away from them. In some cases, they evolve from campus fraternities. They are led by local 'warlords', operating at the street, community or ethnic level, with ties to member of the ruling elite, who deploy them for a mix of political and quasi-criminal activities, including oil theft. Examples include Dee Gbam, De Well, Bush Boys, Icelanders, and the Niger Delta vigilantes (NDV). Criminal armed groups exist basically for self-enrichment and engage in violent crimes. It should still be noted that IKelegbe's categories, though useful, are not exhaustive, as individuals and groups flow across the boundaries between one category and the other, based on exigent calculations and complex in group dynamics that are difficult to capture.

DYNAMIC OF RESISTANCE POLITICS AND CONFLICT

To illustrate this point, in 1999, three Niger Delta state governors were able to penetrate and sponsor some of these armed groups in the region to unleash violence upon, and intimidate their political opponents and voters. Of note was the governor of Rivers state, who got two of the leaders of such groups – Mujaheed Asari Dokubo (later, with the governor's support, president of the IYC) and Ateke Tom (then leader of the Okrika Vigilante, later Niger Delta vigilantes) – to 'help' him during the 1999 and 2003 elections (Best and Kemedi, 2005; Manby, 2004). However, after winning power, the politicians abandoned these armed groups. Asari and Ateke were believed to have turned to the transnational illegal oil bunkering networks, collecting tolls on the trade, providing security to oil bunkering crews, selling stolen oil, or operating illegal oil refineries whose products were sold below market prices.

By involving themselves in illegal oil bunkering and getting payoffs from local political patrons or oil companies, militia leaders gained access to funds with which they stockpiled sophisticated weapons, built camps, and recruited and trained fighters. They also gained autonomy from their erstwhile political patrons, giving them space to pursue alternative agendas. Of note in this regard was Asari Dokubo, who in 2003 broke off his association with Governor Odili, whom he accused of "rigging the 2003 elections in Rivers state", and formed the Niger Delta Peoples Volunteer Force (NDPVF), ostensibly to fight for Ijaw right (Manby 2004). A year later bloody conflict ensued between NDPVF and NDV, with the latter believed to be backed by the state government seeking to destroy Asari's influence, particularly after he adopted populist rhetoric in promoting his credentials as a defender of Ijaw ethnic minority rights. Shortly after, he and Ateke signed a peace agreement facilitated by mediators in Abuja in October 2004.

It is believed that some prominent politicians and governors of two other Niger Delta states, Bayelsa and Delta, had links with some of the militias in their domains and used them in rigging elections among other things. In some parts of Delta, militia and gang leaders were indirectly paid by oil companies and installations to protect oil installations, and fight against community associations or individuals who were disturbing oil operations.

DYNAMIC OF RESISTANCE POLITICS AND CONFLICT

7.1 MEND: The Militarization of Resistance

The most potent militant group engaging in local resistance, but targeting a global audience is the Movement for the Emancipation of the Niger Delta (MEND). As a coalition of Ijaw armed groups across the region, MEND itself has not been free of factionalization (Obi 2008:425), even if a core group has reminded fairly consistent in its methods and principles. MEND is believed to have been formed between December 2005 and January 2006. On January 11, 2006, it attacked the East Area (EA) oil field off the Niger Delta coast, abducting four oil workers who were held for 19 days (Obi 2008:60). It had its roots in a loose, pan-Delta coalition, including the Federated Niger Delta Ijaw Communities (FNDIC), the Niger Delta Peoples Volunteer Force (NDPVF), and other armed groups from Delta, Bayelsa, and Rivers states (Ukiwo 2007;

Okonte 2007; Coventry Cathedral 2009:123-124). MEND decided to strike again in February 2006, after an attack by the JTF on Okerenkoko in the Ijaw clan of the Western Delta ostensibly to put an end to the activities of illegal oil bunkerers. This time, MEND fighters attacked "Shell's flow platform, leading to a significant reduction in Nigeria's oil production" (Obi 2008:61).

Since then, the group has attracted international attention to the plight of the Ijaw and its resistance campaign by taking foreign oil workers hostage, demonstrating the inability of Nigerian security forces to stop its attacks and sabotage of oil installations through the effective use of the global news media. By sending emails and pictures to the world's leading news agencies and local newspapers, and by taking journalist to its camps in the swamps of the Niger Delta (Junger 2007),MEND has tried to distance itself from, and has criticized, the Niger Delta faction of the ruling elite as well as opportunistic criminal gangs posing as militants. The movements has also tapped into Ijaw traditional beliefs and sense of collective grievance to gain legitimacy and give voice to its demand for resource control and social injustice. It has however, gained most attention by its threats to "cripple Nigerian oil exports" (IRIN 2006).

DYNAMIC OF RESISTANCE POLITICS AND CONFLICT

MEND has been profiled by The Memorial Institute for

the Prevention of Terrorism (MIPT) (MIPT 2007) as "an active terrorist group that uses violent means to support the rights of the ethnic Ijaw people in the Niger Delta". This profile dwells more on labeling than analyzing the circumstances within which MEND emerged and the content of its messages. It aims at constructing the appearance of an imminent 'terrorist threat' to western energy interests that may appeal to some corporate / state actors, when what is called for is a more nuanced and informed view of MEND. Such a reading will locate MEND's emergence in "the lethal cocktail of economic deprivation, military dictatorship and worsening environmental crisis" in the Niger Delta, and its tapping into " the fifty year Ijaw quest for social and environmental justice in the Niger Delta" (Okonta 2007: 7-71). While MEND has abducted foreign oil workers, it has released all such hostages after a period, all unharmed hostages are used to draw international attention to its cause and to put pressure on the state-oil multinationals alliance. In an interview with Brain Ross, Jomo Gbomo, the spokesperson of MEND, elucidated the objectives of the group:

> *The movement for the Emancipation of the Niger Delta (MEND) is an amalgam of all armed bearing groups in the Niger Delta fighting for the control of oil revenue by indigenes of the Niger Delta who have had relatively no benefits from the exploitation*

> *of our mineral resources by the Nigerian government and oil companies over the last fifty years (Ross 2007).*

MEND's violent campaign against the government and the oil multinationals has been based on the tactical use of surprise attacks on strategic oil installations linked to production and exports, secrecy surrounding the identity of its core operators and a sophisticated media campaign. Although the militant group has been affected by factionalism, its public face, represented by emails to the media, by Jomo Sobomo, has remained consistent in articulating the tenets of its campaign. It has also cooperated with pan-Delta groups such as the Martyrs Brigade, Coalition for Militant Action in the Niger Delta (COMA), and the Joint Revolutionary Council (JRC). There was confrontation between MEND and the military which occurred against the background of two JTF attack on the communities of Oporoza and Okerenkoko in Gbaramantu Kingdom in the Western Delta on May 13, 2009, followed by the destruction of the militia camps, including the strategic camp 5, belonging to militia leader Government Ekpemupolo , alias Tompolo, once associated with MEND.

DYNAMIC OF RESISTANCE POLITICS AND CONFLICT

MEND responded through increased rhetoric against the state-oil alliance in the media and retaliatory attacks on strategic oil pipelines in the Niger Delta that largely crippled the operations of all transnationals – Shell, Chevron, Texaco, and Agip in the Niger Delta (Nwachukwu and Ekot 2009; Ebiri and Etim 2009; Ume and Uwuyiaren 2009 etc). In addition, MEND made the release of one of its detained leaders, Henry Okah, a condition for a ceasefire. Under pressure domestically and internationally, the Nigerian government announced an amnesty to fighters willing to lay down their arms and freed Okah . This fulfilled one of the conditions for dialogue with the government. In spite of this, MEND carried out its first attack outside the Niger Delta, blowing up the Atlas core oil jetty in Lagos, the main distribution source for refined petroleum products to south west Nigeria, on the eve before Okah's release on July 13, after which its ceasefire held.

Several developments have been instrumental to the mid-2009 situation in the region: the submission of the report of the technical committee on the Niger Delta to the federal government, the establishment of the federal ministry of the Niger Delta, and the announcement by the federal government on June 23, 2009, of an amnesty for all militants who renounce armed struggle and lay down their arms. More will be highlighted on the amnesty program of the Federal Government in next chapter. Also of note was the released of the MEND leader, Henry Okah, leading to the declaration of a

60-day cease-fire by MEND effective from July 15, 2009. The reality that MEND reflects a mix of several tendencies, ranging from radical resistance to its ambivalence toward the Niger Delta ruling elite, makes it rather difficult to predict the prospects for the struggle in the Niger Delta after Okah's release. Indications suggest that the extent to which his release will influence developments on the ground will depend on the balance of power between the various factions – ideologues, political activists, and fighting units within MEND – and the attitude and policies of the Federal Government, the Niger Delta state governors, and the ruling elite. It should be noted here that Henry Okah, after his release left to South Africa where he was alleged to have masterminded Abuja bombing of October 14, 2010 and his subsequent detention and trial for terrorism in that country. However, having been mobilized into violent resistance and in the face of such very high stakes, MEND is unlikely to retreat without wresting major concessions that would require the state-transnational oil alliance to address the roots of the Niger Delta conflict. In fact while some MEND "ex-commanders" , such as Ebikabowei Victor Ben ("General" Boyloaf) and Kile Selky Torughedi ("Young Shall Grow"), or factions may be co-opted by government or ruling elites, the core group in MEND have continued to mobilize violence and continue its campaign for resource control and "true fiscal federalism" (Reuters 2009). This is however, evidence in recent attack on an oil pipeline at Brass, Bayelsa state. In a statement signed by the group's spokesperson, Jomo Gbomo, and sent to some media houses via electronic mail, MEND explained that the attack on Agip trunk line was a reminder that its men were still in the creeks. The MEND statement reads in part, "on- Saturday the 4th of February 2012 at 19:30hrs, fighters of the movement for the Emancipation of the Niger Delta attacked and destroyed the Agip trunk line at Brass in Bayelsa state in the Niger Delta region of Nigeria. This relatively insignificantly attack is a reminder of our presence in the creeks of the Niger Delta and a sign of things to come. In this new phase of our struggle for Justice, the movement for the Emancipation of the Niger Delta (MEND) will pay considerable attention to dealing with security forces and traitorous indigenes of the Niger Delta". Chidi Orazulike: www.nigerianoilgas.com – 29/02/2012.

DYNAMIC OF RESISTANCE POLITICS AND CONFLICT

ENE UDIOKO

NIGER DELTA CRISIS: EFFECT ON WOMEN

114

CHAPTER EIGHT

NIGER DELTA CRISIS: EFFECT ON WOMEN

Women suffer great hardships in times of conflict. The women of the Niger Delta are no exception. During the conflicts with oil companies and the Nigerian government, women are subjected to all kind of violence – sexual – such as rape, physical violence such as beatings, maiming – Murder, and destruction of properties. Niger Delta women suffer unimaginable human rights abuses for which redress is unattainable because the agents of government who perpetrate the abuses cannot be subjected to the rule of law. Husbands, fathers and sons have been killed or maimed in the conflict and women have had to assume burdens of home responsibilities as heads of house- holds. This group of people bear the brunt of injustice. The most and worse still, the sufferings of these women often pass unnoticed unless when they protest and threaten to go naked. Even at that, lips promises are made and the problem still remains. Why must women of Niger Delta protest or threaten striping before getting the basic infrastructure/amenities – electricity, water, education, employment for themselves, for their husbands and children which are the basic human rights in other parts of the world?

Even though the Niger Delta is described by many authors as the "goose that lays Nigeria's golden egg", the deprivation the people are experiencing in the region is alarming and women seem to be at the receiving end. This should worry both the international and national consciences.

NIGER DELTA CRISIS: EFFECT ON WOMEN

Rape and Prostitution

In a chaotic situation like that existing in the Niger Delta area, rape and prostitution are common. First of all, the angry and hungry young men who are fighting for their rights will make do with any woman around. Secondly, the soldiers usually sent by the federal government to calm the rioting villagers use the women in the area as their resting place. At night, they invade private homes, terrorized residents with beatings and raping women and girls. Thirdly, girls and young women who are looking for economic survival hang around the oil companies and keep themselves at the service of both the national and international oil workers who are believed to be 'guys in money'. These women are given few Naira or at most few dollars at the end of every sexual meeting. It is clear then that staff of the multinationals are not only enjoying cheap labor but they also have cheap sex at their disposition. Worse still, most of these relationships end up with children and the women are left alone to carry the burden of bringing up these "fatherless babies. In fact, the association of Niger Delta Women for Justice (NDWJ) has been fighting for a law making it mandatory for the oil workers especially foreigners to claim their offspring and if possible the mothers of such children born out of any of the company's staff's promiscuous activities.

8.1   The Women of the Niger Delta

As with women in other parts of the globe, Niger Delta Women retain certain economic responsibilities within the family as wives, mothers and farmers. First of all, they are the principal care-givers of their children and the aged. Even though they are the "food producers, procurers and preparers", they are also expected to be significant wage earners. This is because the intra-household income distribution patterns and the rise of women-headed household in Nigeria, coupled with servile poverty, forces them to take active financial role in their families since most of them are uneducated and therefore unemployed outside the home, their main source of income is agriculture where they "Comprise 60-80 percent of the agricultural labor force and account for 90 percent of family food supply". Leitth-Ross argues that Nigerian women, because of their economic importance as mothers, farm cultivators and traders, have been rather more powerful than is generally thought". As a result of these responsibilities, the Niger Delta women are always willing to fight any unfavorable condition to the realization of these duties, hence their struggle against degradation of any sort.

NIGER DELTA CRISIS: EFFECT ON WOMEN

8.2   Their Struggles and Protests

Chronologically, mass community protests against multinationals began with the Ogharefe women's protest in 1984 against U.S. Pan Ocean. As we shall see later, in each of the protest, the women's objectives were simple and their demands clear and right: Oil companies and their god-fathers must make concrete efforts to improve the economic, environmental, and social conditions of the rural communities – their hosts. In effect, they demanded that their youths and husbands be employed as a way of giving them some sense of belonging. They also requested the provisions of social amenities such as good roads, water, health care facilities and electricity supply to enhance their standard of living.

As already mentioned, in 1984 and 1986, women in Warri mobilized and protested against oil companies. They demanded that the oil companies should pay them for lands seized and pollution damage. When Pan Ocean refused to compensate the people for acquired lands used as oil fields or even pay for millions of dollars worth of crude it explores daily, groups of women rose against this company and laid siege to it. They halted production through dance, song and the threat of nakedness in an effort to restore their community's economic, environmental and social security. After this protest, community action against the state and multinationals increased with a series of mass protests demanding economic, political and social justice.

That was why in 1999 the same scene repeated itself but this time against Shell. That year, to make matter worse, the Niger Delta women and their allies staged simultaneous protests in Nigeria and London against dangerous burning of natural gas by the oil companies. In Nigeria, the women and allied men blocked the shell oil stations, while in London, thirteen activists occupied shell headquarters. They barricaded themselves in the managing director's offices and broadcasted to the outside via digital cameras, laptop computers and mobile phones.

NIGER DELTA CRISIS: EFFECT ON WOMEN

Then come the turn of Chevron in 2002. This could be considered the most serious of all women uprising in the region because of the amount of international media attention it received, the long duration – 10 days and above all, the women threatened to strip – most natural and powerful way of getting their message across but on unthinkable gesture in the West. Led by the women of the Ijaw and Itsekiri communities, angry at the unemployment of their children and husbands, lack of infrastructure and economic empowerment by the federal government and multinational oil companies, two to three hundred women occupied Chevron's exploration site. Around the same time, women from Ilaje and also some other from Ijaw and Itsekiri paralyzed activities at the operational headquarters of Shell Petroleum Development Corporation (SPDC). Here again, the women asked that the multinationals should see to the electrification, foreshore walls, and housing projects in the nine host communities to improve the environmental and living conditions there.

To convince the women to call off the occupation, Chevron reached its usual lips agreement with the women pledging to improve sanitation, electrify villages and build schools, clinics and town halls. They also promised to employ 25 locals for five years and to build poultries and fish farms. The literature so far reviewed show that these promises were not kept, no wonder the women took to the site the following year 2003. As already mentioned, after all the protests and the never-fulfilled promises on the part of the Nigerian government and its accomplice, the multinationals, nothing had changed. The condition of things in the region became worse than before. In reaction to this deplorable state, about 600 women, young and old took to the oil sites one more time, taking hostage of about 700 oil workers from different nationalities. As were in the previous demonstrations, all they wanted was for the oil companies to give employment to their husbands, children and some of the oil riches for the development of the Niger Delta most of which, as we have seen so far, have no basic amenities and infrastructure. It is however, regrettable that things are the way they are because of bad political system – especially the selfish and unjust control of the oil revenue on the part of the Nigerian government and the multinational oil companies.

NIGER DELTA CRISIS: EFFECT ON WOMEN

8.3   Fuelling the Violence in Niger Delta

The Under-discussed factors contributed in no small measures in fuelling violence in the Niger Delta.

Illegal Arms:

Non-state forces have accessed illicit international arms markets since 2003, leading to significant escalation in the sophistication and volume of importation of weapons in early 2006. Through multiple channels of supply, sophisticated weapons are widely available throughout the Niger Delta. Militia groups, cult groups and gangs have sufficient firepower to seriously challenge the authority of Nigeria's Military and police forces. Lagos has featured as a major clearing port for illegal small arms with the complicity of customs officers. Similarly, weapons have been landed at Niger Delta ports with the knowledge and complicity of senior State Security Officers. Local illicit arms dealers use Niger Delta ports to import weapons through import-export business, and then distribute the weapons through their state networks, particularly in Akwa Ibom and Anambra States. It is alleged that military personnel have been involved in supplying weapons from Nigerian Military armories. Training camps led by ex-military officers were functioning in strategic locations throughout the Niger Delta in 2006 before the amnesty program of the federal government.

Arms were also conveyed through illegal oil bunkering, often as part payment for smuggled oil. Oil companies and state governments also provided payments for "security services" to ensure that oil operations are permitted to continue without disturbance. Such payments are often used by disaffected youth to improve their arsenals. The number of illegal small arms seized by Nigeria's customs is tiny. Weapons seizures at border points known to be key ports of entry for shipments of illegal arms such as Lagos and Port Harcourt are almost unknown. Similarly recovery of illegal arms by the Nigerian military and police is negligible.

The source countries of weapons illegally imported into Nigeria include all bordering countries (Benin, Cameroon, Chad and Niger). Weapons are illegally procured through Cameroon, often as part of shipment of machinery parts or smuggled inside petrol tankers. Other reported countries from which illegal weapons and ammunition are sourced include Cote d'voire, Liberia, South Africa, Turkey, and Ukraine, as well as Bulgaria, Kosovo, and Serbia. Weapons decommissioned by the military have been shipped from the Ukraine through Odessa and Dubai. In one document instance, a Greek vessel under a Liberian flag was used, with on-shipment by former KGB Major Victor Bout's fleet of Antonous from Sharjah airfield (Dubai), With the arrest of Bout, arguably the most prominent international dealer known to have connections with the supply of illicit arms in West Africa, there is an opportunity to seriously disrupt and constrain the flow of weapons into Nigeria. The key driver is political will to enforce interdiction and prosecution as well as to engage with international agencies.

Unemployment:

Nigeria's oil industry employs only about 30,000 workers, satisfying virtually none of the local demands for jobs. The general poverty and under-development of the region offers little basis for livelihoods, especially for young men. Over the years there has been a steady drift of youth from rural areas to major population centers such as Port Harcourt. Increasing numbers of youth are faced with poverty rather than the expected prosperity of the city. The financial benefits from the illicit activities of street gangs, cult groups and militia, serve to perpetuate criminality and social disintegration, especially in a context of weak law enforcement and corrupt authorities.

NIGER DELTA CRISIS: EFFECT ON WOMEN

Social Disintegration:

Social disintegration is seen in the loss of legitimacy by elders and community leaders, the loss of livelihoods in farming and fishing settlements, the displacement of communities, rising ethnic antagonism and the rise of violence and criminality among youth. The destruction of robust social structures with their inherent control mechanisms means there are few constraints on behaviors, or local mechanisms for reining in conflict. This deterioration feeds the cycle of unemployment, poverty, any reasonable back-up to rebuild social fabric, or to sustain alternative controls to stabilize society. Rather, the state responds only when the system is evidently out of control. The response is usually in the form of impulsive and brutal military action which serves to exacerbate the situation.

Oppressive, violent action further undermines stability and social control.

Corruption:

Pervasive corruption within the government, oil companies, and even some non-governmental organizations (NGOs), prevents the delivery of funds intended for infrastructure and community development. Bribery, embezzlement, fraud and other vices have gained root in most public offices and permeate the private sector. Money laundering and advanced fee fraud - often referred to as '419' (so named after Section 419 of the Criminal Code) are offshoots of this malaise. Corruption relationships foster the diversion of revenues which aggravate grievances among the communities of the Delta. Rampant corruption has also destroyed respect for social order. At a community and inter-community level, suspicion and tension emerging from oil sector-related corruption drives conflict. At regional level, corruption maintains systemic poverty and inequality, which forms an important catalyst of instability.

NIGER DELTA CRISIS: EFFECT ON WOMEN

Political interference and bribery reduce public confidence in the courts and legal system. Collusion among criminals and state security forces renders law enforcement largely ineffective in dealing with oil theft. Militia activity could not flourish without corruption. A sustained attack on corruption, including successful prosecutions, is required to break the nexus of illegal arms, oil theft and money laundering. This would build public confidence and trust in government, enabling any peace agreement reached among the parties to have a greater chance of success.

MULTINATIONAL COMPANIES (MNCs): WHAT THEY ARE

CHAPTER NINE

MULTINATIONAL COMPANIES
(MNCs): WHAT THEY ARE

In an attempt to understand what a multi-national company (MNC) is all about, experts give varying emphasis to its definition. What is important to note is that these experts do accept that the existence of international capital market followed by international flow of knowledge has widely aided the establishment of a business enterprise in more than one originating country (Dunning 1994; Vernon, 1977; Turner 1973; Jacoby 1975 etc). Thus a multinational company or corporation (MNC) is simply defined by Dunning (1974:13), as a business enterprise which owns and controls income generating assets in more than one country. Putting it differently, we can say that MNC is an enterprise or firm with its headquarters in a developed country and its branches in other developing and developed countries. Broadly speaking, a MNC is a firm with branches or subsidiaries in more than one country. The degree of foreign operation in such a case, can be measured by the proportion of the foreign content of its total assets, employment, products or sales (Wilezynski, 1976; Duru, 1999). Linked with this is the fact that MNCs as observed by Vernon (1977) have always been distinguished in the public mind by their sheer size; they are, far the most part, the giants of modern industry, commerce and banking. As further indicated by Vernon, the MNC size (that size should not fall below Us $100 million as at 1977) and geographical spread are among the important characteristics. Another characteristics of a MNC considered central has to do with profit maximization effort which focuses not for its individual subsidiaries but rather for the centre parent company.

So far, attempts have been made to explain what a MNC is all about. Regrettably, there is no universal agreement as to its meaning. But usually, experts believe multinationals to be those companies that have productive facilities in many lands, have access to capital world-wide and have a global outlook among their management. As advanced by Boarman (1977) and Duru (1999), other distinguishing features which facilitate the successful operations of MNCs in host countries are enormous resources at their disposal, managerial skills and entrepreneurial abilities.

MULTINATIONAL COMPANIES (MNCs): WHAT THEY ARE

In terms of market structure, most MNCs are oligopolies, not at all absolute identical products but with differentiated brands / names (Ndebbio, 1988; Leftwich, 1976). An oligopolistic firm or a MNC is expected to share the control of the industry or market with a few other firms. In economics, we have tight and loose oligopoly. Under tight oligopoly, firms involved should not normally exceed ten in number (in the US, 5-6 firms) to enable them practice effective collusion, while under loose, firm can exceed ten as they are not expected to succeed in practicing effective collusion either to increase or decrease prices of their products, among other things. In Nigeria, for instance the petroleum industry with about eight firms, namely Shell and Total, is Oligopolistic in nature and tight control is displayed by the petroleum/oil firms in the industry. On the other hand, the beer brewing industry with more than 20 firms in Nigeria is also Oligopolistic in nature but exhibits loose control over member firms. It should be noted that these oil firms in Nigeria are controlled by oil MNCs from different developed countries.

9.2   Benefits and Costs of MNCS

In an attempt to explain the benefits and costs associated with MNCs in developing countries, fundamental questions have been asked and debated upon by scholars including Streeten (1974), Behrman(1960), Akinsanya (1980), etc. These questions, among others include (i) Do the benefits generally of MNCs outweigh costs sustained by the host countries? (ii) Do the contributions of MNCs to economic development of the host countries outweigh the costs to these economies? (iii) what are the social and political consequences of the operations of MNCs in most developing host countries? (iv) Do MNCs behave as a threat to national sovereignty as well as instruments of foreign domination and dependency? Empirically, some of the above questions can be examined using the index of foreign private investment (FPI) or foreign direct investment (FDI) as indicated in the works of Penrose (1974), Streeten (1974), Nyong, (2000), etc. If the existence of MNCs in the host countries can produce higher net in-flow of FPI than the net out-flow, it could then be said that benefits would out-weigh costs provided the additional investments realized are productively put to use.

MULTINATIONAL COMPANIES (MNCs): WHAT THEY ARE

At this juncture, it is important to identify the two schools of thought involved in the debate as to whether or not MNCs are beneficial to the developing host countries. The first group is the liberal capitalist school, otherwise referred to as the complementary hypothesis school. This school postulates that foreign capital in flow is beneficial to economic development in the less development countries (LDCs) by complementing the low savings in these countries, increasing the pool of financial resource available for productive investment, and overcoming technological backwardness. As productive investment increase, growth and development will be achieved. Thus, foreign capital inflow is a sine-qua-non for rapid development and LDCs should encourage MNCs through appropriate policies not to always repatriate their income. The second group is the substitution hypothesis school of thought fashioned along the traditional views of Marxian-Leninist orientation. This school disagrees with the liberal capitalist school of thought. As captured in Nyong's work; the proponents of this school maintain that foreign capital inflows and MNCs rather than act as a complement to domestic savings, operate to discourage domestic savings and hence perpetuate and widen economic inequality between the rich and the poor.

MULTINATIONAL COMPANIES (MNCs): WHAT THEY ARE

9.3 **Benefits**

For the benefits side, the proponent particularly those of liberal capitalist school, argue that MNCs are socially describable because they have a net increase in income or output, in capital formation, in employment, in government tax revenue and in technological transfer. In the case of net increase in income, MNCs can help in filling, both the savings and foreign exchange gaps (commonly referred to as the two gap model of the neoclassical strand) through massive importation of foreign capital. With the substantial reduction of these gaps and proper utilization of foreign capital, LDCs can achieve rapid economic growth and escape the vicious cycle of poverty. On the issue of employment generation and increase in productivity, it is common knowledge that MNCs do employ local staff and pay higher wages than existing wages in the rural sector, thus helping to increase employment and raise productivity of local labor. From the company income tax and royalties (from concession agreements) paid by MNCs, government tax revenue increased. Therefore, the federal government earns more revenue through oil MNCs as in the case of Nigeria. In the case of technological transfer; MNCs do not only provide finance, they also provide managerial, administrative and technical personnel, new technology, research and innovations in new products, all of which are in short supply in the LDCs. In most cases, the training of technical personnel from among local nationals by the MNCs is done for lower and middle level positions.

9.4   Costs

Costs or disadvantages of MNCs and Foreign Private Investment (FPI) on host LDCs have been generally identified mostly by the proponents of substitution hypothesis school of thought. The costs are listed as follows:

1. Lopsided infrastructural development.
2. Deterioration in terms of trade and balance of payments.
3. Large reduction in government revenue. This could result from an attempt to encourage FPI and usually it takes the form of excessive tax concessions which in turn will cause a substantial fall in government revenue.

4. Limited technology transfer and technological dependency.
5. Transfer pricing malpractices. By transfer pricing, we mean the price charged by one subsidiary of a company for goods supplied by another subsidiary. The malpractice occurs when a multinational company (MNC) raises the prices of goods transferred to its subsidiary from other

subsidiaries. Obviously, this will lead to a reduction of consumer's surplus.

6. Limited employment generation. This is due to the fact that most MNCs reserve substantial senior positions for their nationals who are paid very high salaries, allowances and benefits. However, MNCs do train local nationals only for middle and lower level positions.

By and large, the costs of MNCs on the host developing countries have been summarized thus:

> *"MNC will accentuate inequalities in the distribution of income because rewards will go to the most productive. They (MNCs) will increase unemployment of the unskilled, for the technology which their use has been developed in societies where labor is scare and capital abundant. They will aggravate regional inequalities, for location of plant in the service of efficiency and this will conflict with regional, provincial or state claims of fair shares. They will accentuate sectorial inequalities and reinforce dualism, for modern technology is suited only for certain types of industrial activities. They will draw on outside resources and men, and will also draw resources and men inside,*

> *guided only by costs and returns, without regard to national sentiments or social needs"* (Streeten, 1974: 242).

MULTINATIONAL COMPANIES (MNCs): WHAT THEY ARE

In spite of the inconclusive debate as to whether MNCs are capable of increasing benefits more than costs and vice versa to the host LDCs, there is a consensus or agreement among advocates and opponents of benefit-cost debate of MNCs. As observed further by Streeten (1974), most advocates and opponents agree that a MNC does indeed serve as a most potent agent of innovation, a ruthless cutter of costs and an expert in harnessing resources. This observation encompasses parent and host countries multinational companies.

9.5 Some Cases of Communities Exploited and Destroyed in Niger Delta for Demanding their Rights

In the Niger Delta region, there are some communities that the oil MNCs has connived with the federal (military) Government to destroy. The refusal of the oil MNCs to meet their social responsibilities has, in most cases, caused the communities to agitate and even riot for their rights. Let us briefly examine a few of these communities here:

(i)   Ogoni community in Rivers State:

The continued neglect of Ogoni community in the Rivers State of the Niger Delta led to the community's protest in which became international against oil MNCs such as Shell. Instead of Shell (SPDC) changing to do what is right for the community, it decided to connive with the federal government headed by the late General Sani Abacha. This connivance led to the execution by Abacha of the protest leaders, namely, Ken Saro-Wiwa and eight other Ogoni leaders in 1995. That was a very terrible happening that has continued to worsen the economic fortune of the community.

(ii)   Iko community in Akwa Ibom:

Iko community in Eastern Obolo L.G.A of Akwa Ibom state also had problems with Shell, the pioneer oil MNC in the early 1990s. Instead of using vertical arrangement of gas flaring, shell decided to use horizontal arrangement of gas flaring. This caused houses in Iko to be destroyed without adequate compensation. The Iko people protested against the neglect and resisted further gas flaring via horizontal arrangement. This particular event has nothing to do with existing land dispute between IKo and Oko Ette.

MULTINATIONAL COMPANIES (MNCs): WHAT THEY ARE

(iii)   Odi

Community in Bayelsa State:

This community also suffered from neglect, deprivation, etc from oil companies operating in the community, and there was a civil disobedience.

Following the directive of President Obasanjo in November 1999, Odi community was inhumanly destroyed.

(iv)   Ikot Ebidan Community in Onah L.G.A of Akwa Ibom State:

There was a property damage caused by Mobil Oil exploration in the 1990s at Ikot Ebidan Community. Compensation was denied those whose properties were damaged. This led to a prompt action by the women of the community who had to riot and close an important bridge in the area.

(v)   Eket Community in Akwa Ibom:

What caused problems was the issue of Mobil Producing Unlimited not willing to hire senior staff members from the core community of Eket, in Akwa Ibom State. The statement by the then military Governor of the State-Adeusi, that the state had no qualified experts to be hired for the petroleum work angered many Akwa Ibomites. This was in 1997/98. There was crisis coupled with some riot which really embarrassed Adeusi, the then Chief Executive of AKS.

So for, we have seen that the refusal of oil multinational corporations to meet the legitimate demands/rights of most communities in the Niger Delta including specifically, the few communities cited above, has produced civil unrest, protest and even riot. In an attempt to quell the protesters, rioters, etc, the federal authorities duly directed and supported by the oil MNCs, caused wanton destruction of these communities. The experiences of the people in most communities of the Niger Delta have been seen to have no means of livelihood. With all what has transpired, one can say that the economic backwardness of the Niger Delta has even been aggravated principally by the oil MNCs in conjunction with the federal authorities.

FED. GOVT. DEVT. EFFORTS INTHE NIGER DELTA

CHAPTER TEN

FEDERAL GOVERNMENT DEVELOPMENT EFFORTS IN THE NIGER DELTA

The Niger Delta Region has witnessed a number of attempts to influence the pace and nature of development in the area and improve the standard of life for its people. For the most part the legacy of these schemes translates into a picture of missed opportunities, low value for money and, not the least, enormous disappointment for the communities of the Niger Delta whose hopes and aspirations have been raised and then repeatedly shattered. This section shall attempt a review of various development responses by the federal government at different periods.

10.1 The Niger Delta Development Board (NDDB)

The unique characteristics of the Niger Delta Region lay behind Sir Henry Willink's Commission (1958) recommendation that the area deserved special developmental attention by the federal government of Nigeria. This was even before crude oil became a critical factor in Nigeria's development. In response, the federal government established the Niger Delta Development Board (NDDB) in 1960 to manage the developmental needs and challenges, of the region. The special area was defined as Yenagoa Province, Degema province, the Ogoni Division of Port-Harcourt and the Western Ijaw Division of Delta province.

In its seven years of existence, however, the NDDB achieved little before it faded away following the military coup in 1966 and the outbreak of civil war in 1967. After the civil way, the NDDB was not revived and the government showed no interest in addressing the developmental needs of the region. Rather, it decided to use the substantial revenue accruing from oil production in the region to fund a massive rehabilitation and reconstruction program in various parts of the country. Even with the quadrupling oil prices in 1973 and the subsequent oil wind fall, there was no deliberate attempt to use part of the oil wealth to address the issue of poverty and the development need of the region.

10.2 Presidential Task Force (the 1.5% Committee)

Following growing agitation for a renewed focus on the development of the region, the 1979/83 Administration set up a presidential task force (popularly known as the 1.5% committee) in 1980 and 1.5% of the federation account was allocated to the committee to tackle the developmental problems of the region. Although the committee existed until early years of the 1985/93 regime, it was largely ineffective. There were only a few projects to show for the funding received from the Federation Account and very little visible beneficial impacts on the welfare of the people of the oil producing communities.

10.3 Oil Mineral Producing Areas Development Commission (OMPADEC)

Following growing discontent and restiveness in the Oil Producing areas, The Babangida regime set up the oil mineral producing areas commission (OMPADEC) in 1992. Three percent of federal oil revenue was allocated to the commission to address the developmental needs of the areas. Although OMPADEC initially raised the spirit and hopes of the people, inefficiency and corruption in the organization resulted in yet more disappointment. Between 1992 and 1999 when it was wound up, OMPADEC completed several projects but bequeathed numerous abandoned or unfinished projects and huge debts. There is no reliable information on the total amount the commission received from the Federation Account, but what is clear is that OMPADEC suffered from lack of focus, inadequate and irregular funding, official profligacy, corruption, excessive political interference, lack of transparency and accountability, and high overhead expenditure. Most of its projects had little to do with poverty reduction and the vast majority of the people did not benefit from its activities. In brief, OMPADEC failed abjectly to abate discontent and restiveness in the region. Given this background, it is hardly surprising that one of the fundamental decisions of former president Obasanjo, soon after his inauguration in May 1999, was to submit a Bill to the National Assembly for the establishment of the Niger Delta Development Commission (NDDC) to replace OMPADEC.

FED. GOVT. DEVT. EFFORTS INTHE NIGER DELTA

10.4 Niger Delta Environmental Survey (NDES)

The Niger Delta Environmental Survey (NDES) was set up to reconcile industry, environment and community interest in the Niger Delta. The initiative was prompted by increasing pressure from rapid deteriorating ecological and economic conditions, social dislocation and tension in the communities, which were not being addressed by polices and action. A study of the region by the

World Bank (1995) warned that:

"An urgent need exists to implement mechanism to protect the life and health of the region's inhabitants and its ecological system from further deterioration"

It was against this backdrop that the Niger Delta environmental Survey (NDES) was initiated in February 1995, by Shell Petroleum Development Company (SPDC) on behalf of its joint partners (NNPC, ELF and AGIP) to undertake an environment study of the region and to provide the required database. The survey is now almost entirely funded by oil companies in Nigeria under the umbrella of the Oil Producers Trade section (OPTS) of the Lagos Chamber of Commerce.

NDES therefore created a steering committee in 1996 and engaged EuroConsult, a Dutch firm as the managing consultants for the execution of:

FED. GOVT. DEVT. EFFORTS IN THE NIGER DELTA

- A Cartographic definition of the Niger Delta.
- An overview and evaluation of existing information and data on the region.
- The identification of major issues to be addressed.
- The identification of additional data re-

quirements, and

- The preparation of a detailed TOR and scope of work to be carried out in phases.

The NDES objective has been:

1. To describe and quantify the renewable and non-renewable resources of the Niger Delta, identify and assess the positive and negative factors of resources use in the area and the manner in which they serve and affect local, regional and national interest;

2. To stimulate pro-actively and encourage relevant stakeholders to address and solve specific current social and environmental problems identified in the course of the survey and propose identified in the course of the survey and propose an indicative plan for future management of the region;

3. To appraise how the present state of the region has evolve over time and assess the present conditions of social and economic underdevelopment; and

4. Generate data and information on the Niger Delta, including the formulating strategies and plans for effective natural management towards the sustainable use of resources in order to protect the

environment and the livelihood of the people in the region.

10.5   Niger Delta Development Commission (NDDC)

The Niger Delta Development Commission (NDDC) is the brainchild of the Nigeria former president Olusegun Obasanjo. Shortly after being sworn into office, Obasanjo followed through with a key pledge he had made earlier during his election campaign. Upon election, he would "seek immediate solution that would bring enduring peace and progress to the people of the Niger Delta" The NDDC was officially inaugurated on December 21, 2000 with a mission "to offer a lasting solution to the social-economic difficulties of the Niger Delta Region" and a mission "to facilitate the rapid, even and sustainable development of the Niger Delta into a region that is economically prosperous, socially stable, ecologically regenerative and politically peaceful".

FED. GOVT. DEVT. EFFORTS IN THE NIGER DELTA

The NDDC Act provided for generous funding sources, including:

- Federal government contribution which was to be equivalent to 15% of the monthly statutory allocation due to member states of the commission from the Federation Account,

- Oil and gas processing companies' contribution of 3% of their total budget.

- 50% of the Ecological Fund Allocations due to the member states

- Proceeds from NDDC Assets and Miscellaneous sources, including grants-in-aid, gifts, loans and donations.

The Act also provides for a governing board of twenty members. Ten of the members are appointed by the federal government (the presidency) including the chairman, the MD/CEO, the two Executive Directors, three Representatives of non-oil producing states, one representative each from the federal ministry of Finance and the Federal Ministry of Environment and one representative of oil companies. Each of the nine oil producing state appoint one member each while the oil companies appoint one member to represent them.

The commission's initial task was to review and complete some of the abandoned / unfinished project of the defunct OMPADEC and embark on some new ones whilst preparing a comprehensive master plan for the development of the Niger Delta region with offices in each of the nine oil producing states, during the first three years of its existence (January 2001 to January 2003), the NDDC:

FED. GOVT. DEVT. EFFORTS IN THE NIGER DELTA

- Received ₦47 billion from oil its funding

sources.

- Awarded about 700 contracts of which 358 had been completed by June 2003.

- Undertook the construction of 40 road projects, 90 water projects, 129 electrification projects,47 shore projection/ jetty projects, 50 health centres, 205 new blocks of six classrooms each.

10.6   **Functions and Powers of the Commission:** The Commission shall:

(a) Formulate policies and guidelines for the development of the Niger Delta area.

(b) Conceive, plan and implement, in accordance with set rules and regulations, projects and programs for the sustainable development of the Niger Delta area in the field of transportation including roads, jetties and waterways, health, education, employment , industrialization, agriculture and fisheries, housing and urban development, ware supply, electricity and telecommunications.

(c)   Cause the Niger Delta area to be surveyed in order to ascertain measures which are necessary to promote its physical and socio-economic development.

(d)   Prepare master plans and schemes designed to promote the physical development of the Niger Delta area and the estimates of the costs of implementing such master plans and schemes.

(e) implement all the measures approved for the development of the Niger Delta area by Federal government and the member states of the commissions.

(f) Identify factors inhibiting the development of the Niger Delta area and assist the member states in the formulation and implementation of policies to ensure sound and efficient management of the resources of the Niger Delta area.

FED. GOVT. DEVT. EFFORTS INTHE NIGER DELTA

(g) Assess and report on any project being funded or carried out in the Niger Delta area by oil and gas producing companies and any other company including non-governmental organizations and ensure that funds released for such projects are properly utilized.

(h) Tackle ecological and environment problems that arise from the exploration of oil mineral in the Niger Delta area and advise the Federal government and the member states on the prevention and control of oil spillages, gas flaring and prevention and environmental pollution.

The functions of NDDC as provided by the Act are nebulous, therefore until the management and board of the commission exercises substantial discretion, the commission may be tempted to do everything and achieve nothing, the implication of carrying out these functions is that the commission has to partner with other agencies, hire the services of contractors and consultants and or interact with other stake holders. For example, the NDDC hired about 32 sector consultants in preparing the master plan, yet till date, the plan has not been fully owned-up by the agencies and peoples of the region. Attempts at establishing a clearing house called partnership for sustainable development (PSD) failed woefully. But even at the monumental failure, NDDC continues without this ritual and rendezvous. The proposed PSD Protocol was rejected by the governors of nine states and even the 185 LGAs are yet to fully buy into it in spite of several attempts at constructive engagement and consultation workshop.

It may be right to observed that the NDDC produced the Niger Delta Regional Development Master Plan, but the claim has been that the modest inputs of stake-holders in the process were not factored-into the finished product. While it is difficult to deny the existence of the master plan, it can be stated without any fear of contradiction that the master plan from conception, crafting to finishing, did not include the people hence it is neither acceptable to the people nor can it be implemented. It is believed that the plan stands on one leg and that it was totally removed from the socio-cultural milieu of the people. The commission is said to have spent several billions of Naira in the crafting process.

FED. GOVT. DEVT. EFFORTS IN THE NIGER DELTA

10.7 Appraisal of the Performance of NDDC

It will be futile to examine the entire development agency in a single chapter. But suffice it to examine a few of the programs of NDDC to ascertain whether or not the commission has done well in the eye of the ordinary people of Niger Delta. Under consideration, are projects that were designed to alleviate poverty, curb youth restiveness and enable the people to create wealth.

(A)   NDDC Quick Impact Projects

In most stakeholders meetings, NDDC had explained why the Master Plan was being crafted. It implemented an interim action in which it embarked on interventionist programs that would have direct and immediate impact on the people. In the interim plan, the commission identified what it called Quick Impact Projects (QIPs) which according to NDDC would accelerate the temps of development in some key sectors of the regional economy. Seven of such QIP area are identified. These include:

- Education or Regional model secondary schools,
- HIV/AIDS and malaria control,

-         Institute of Good Governance and Sustainable Development,
-         Agriculture
-         Micro and Small Business Development,
-         Sports Development, and
-         Power supply and Energy

The commission could not deliver in any of these Quick Impact Projects. These are areas that could have had direct bearing on the lives of the ordinary Niger Delta people. NDDC's score card in the education QIP is perhaps the worst. In May 2005, the Technical Committee on Education was mandated to do valuation work and financial estimates were worked out. The model schools were billed to take-off in September 2005, but the date was put forward to 2006. Unfortunately, till date NDDC has not even one Model Secondary Schools in spite of engaging professional consultants in that regard. The effort and money spent on the QIPs is a monumental waste.

FED. GOVT. DEVT. EFFORTS IN THE NIGER DELTA

(B)   **The NDDC Mass Transit Scheme**

NDDC procures buses and the intention was to give out these vehicles, give them out on hire purchase to the public. Sadly, while the commission procured the wrong type of buses considering the nature of the Nigerian roads, the project was hijacked by those who administered it. What became the practice was for NDDC principal officers to own as many of the buses as possible and then give them out to drivers who had to work themselves out to pay a balance of N7000.00 per day. The result was that in less than two years of its operation more than one-quarter of the buses were either destroyed or abandoned. The Mass Transit Scheme was conceived to alleviate poverty but it led to the aggravation of the scourge for the ordinary Niger Delta people.

(C)   The NDDC / Glo Empowerment Scheme

This was another grand deception designed to create a false impression of empowering the ordinary people. NDDC entered into a Multi-billion Naira partnership with Glo Nigeria Limited. Initially expectations were very high but what did the commissioner deliver? A handful of youths, mostly relatives of NDDC staff were listed and each was given a starter pack of Acatel GSM worth about N6,000.00, an umbrella, two plastic chairs and a table. The empowerment program was so ridiculous that some youths sold the entire starter pack for less than N9,000.00 and spent the money on alcoholic beverages at the commission's gate.

(D)   NDDC NTAC Contracts

The Niger Delta Technical Aid Corp, NTAC Projects, which are capacity building programs for graduates have been grossly mismanaged. The integral part of NTAC projects is computer training programs. Till date the commission is alleged to be indebted to NTAC because the funds for defraying the fees are lodged in private accounts to yield interest for the account holders. At the inauguration of the present Board, Mr. President said unequivocal that "Government needs a technocrat as the managing Director in NDDC to inject seriousness, focus and professionalism in handling the affairs of the Commission, to effectively position it as an intermediary organ to follow up the presidential vision". This presidential vision appears to have been negated. In the 2010 fiscal year, 28 jobs were given to Bayelsa state to tender for, and these are jobs under N250 million. Unfortunately, 19 out of the 28 jobs were given out from the commission without the knowledge of the state commissioner while only 9 jobs were given to the state concerned. Other state commissioners made similar complaints. Actions of this type erode the powers and undermine the integrity of the Board.

FED. GOVT. DEVT. EFFORTS IN THE NIGER DELTA

From the few projects and programs mounted by the commission, the verdict has been that, within the limits of financial constraints, NDDC failed woefully to execute those programs that would have yielded positive results in the life of the ordinary Niger Delta people. The commission is alleged to focus on big projects that will satisfy contractors rather than the ordinary people of Niger Delta.

10.8   Challenges Facing the NDDC

■   **Leadership Challenges**

Self-aggrandizement of the top shots of NDDC, as they are always jostling to benefit from contracts, when the leaders of an organization place their interest first before the overall interest, the people's interest will definitely be sacrificed on the golgotha of self-interest. Because of such poor impression created by the leaders, most people sees the commission as a mere contract awarding agency. As it is a common knowledge that every contractor aims at maximizing profit, it is difficult to understand the use of terminologies as QIPs, master plan, partnership for sustainable development and so on. This is the major challenge the commission is facing in trying to sell the Master plan to stakeholders. In trying to do everything ranging from mass transit; dust bins; glo-starter packs; fishing equipment; school furniture to cassava farms, demonstrates lack of focus and in so doing, available resources are thinly spread without critical mass and lack of specialization.

FED. GOVT. DEVT. EFFORTS IN THE NIGER DELTA

■

Violation of the Act Establishing the Commission

The Managing Director (MD) has consistently flouted and brazenly violated parts of the Act establishing the Commission. Incidents of such violations are legion and deliberate. They range from the award of contacts without due process; non-implementation of the Board's decisions, undue interference with the statutory functions of state representatives to creating a due process unit which is used as an excuse to perpetrate heinous financial crimes in the commission.

Creeping Usurpation of the Functions of the Board

The Board shall have power to: (a) Manage and supervise affairs of the Commission; (b) Make rules and regulations for carrying out the functions of the commission; (c) Enter and inspect premises, projects and such places as may be necessary for the purposes of carrying out its functions under this Act; etc. In the recent past, there was undue interference in the affairs of NDDC by the office of the secretary to the Federal government. As one state commissioner describes it "the office kills every viable program and policy initiatives by the Board and stifles their implementation. It ridicules the decisions of the Board by permitting NDDC contract award letters to be flaunted outside the commission and sole cheaply to contractors". These reports point to the fact that there have been flagrant abuses of contract procedures and due process in the commission.

It should be noted that state offices of the NDDC were created out of necessity for the proper coordination of state projects and to create employment opportunities for the people. Sadly, however, state offices are not being run effectively now because of politics. Frequent conflict between the management and the state commissioners and this negatively affects policy implementation in the states. There are allegations that while management is most inclined to use federal government circulars and memos to administer the commission; the board insists that management should make reference to the NDDC Act in matters concerning administration. There is disconnect between the board and management and this has culminated in mutual antagonism, distrust and high wire politics – all these stifle initiative and productivity of the staff.

FED. GOVT. DEVT. EFFORTS IN THE NIGER DELTA

Offi-cial corruption: over-invoicing and the use of cronies.

The public procurement law of 2007 also applies to the NDDC. It is public knowledge that the Due Process unit has been empowered to draft contract agreements, whereas the commission has a legal department. This process negates bidding and open tendering process. The impression being created is that most Niger Deltans believe that NDDC contracts are given to only those who are politically connected; hence they do not make serious efforts to secure jobs. The conditions for tendering and bidding are so harsh that not many Niger Deltans can meet them. It therefore implies that NDDC contracts are indirectly meant for people outside the region. One of the conditions is that contractors will not obtain mobilization and are expected to deliver on the first milestone.

Investigation indicated that these harsh conditions were unilaterally introduced by the management without the approval of the board.

Contradictions in the NDDC has inherent contradictions, some of which are highlighted below:

Part III, (II) 2 States that the Advisory committee shall be charged with the responsibility of advising the Board and monitoring the activities of the constitution, with a view to achieving the objectives of the commission. The advisory committee has never been seen to play any significant role in NDDC. This is referred to as the another layer of inefficiency which must not be funded. This weakens the control mechanism of the managing director and other executive directors of the commission. The federal government has not been very committed in the release of funds due the commission. While the MNCs can be said to be doing their best the same cannot be said of the federal government. Part V (14), b 3 percent of the total annual budget of any oil producer's company operating on-shore and off-shore, in the Niger Delta shall be credited to NDDC.

Languid

Budgetary Procedure

The NDDC's recurrent expenditure is too high. The gestation period between the award of contracts and their completion time gives rise to project cost-overrun because the payment system is done in milestones, which creates room for the upward review of contract values. It is therefore difficult for even external auditors to detect cases of fraud in respect over-inflation of contract values. There are projects that have occurred and reoccurred in the NDDC for five years without being completed. NDDC's budgets, in the formative years such as two to six years have always been unrealistic budget. The attitude of the federal government in releasing allocations to the commission does not help matters. In NDDC's budgetary process, the federal government through the National Assembly exercises an overbearing influence.

Lack of Focus

In the eyes of the ordinary Niger Deltans, NDDC has become a jack of all trades and master of none. The commission embarks upon any project ranging from the building of six classroom blocks; cottage hospitals; provision of laboratory equipment, building of bridges, construction of roads, canalization, rural electrification to the provision of potable water. The inability of the commission to concentrate on a few areas results in wasted efforts.

Persistent Internal Crisis

For the better part, NDDC has become a theatre of interminable crises. When there is conflict within the commission, such conflicts are sometimes allowed to snowball into a crisis level and they often attract robust media attention. Inability on the part of principal officers to resolve inherent conflicts within the NDDC creates several windows for politicians to exploit.

THE MINISTRY OF NIGER DELTA AFFAIRS

CHAPTER ELEVEN

THE MINISTRY OF NIGER DELTA AFFAIRS

The establishment of the Ministry of Niger Delta Affairs some few years ago by the late President Umaru Yar'Adua was greeted with mixed feelings by some Nigerians. Whereas some people hailed the move as a step in the right direction bearing in mind the difficult terrain of the region which should require a special attention, others however, believed that the creation of the Ministry would unnecessarily slow down the pace of development in the Niger Delta region because of bureaucratic bottlenecks. Those who held the latter view felt that since the creation of the ministry was a mere political gesture to placate the people of the region, its operations would be bedeviled by the bureaucratic hiccups that usually trial government establishments. Perhaps their fears have not been misguided thus far.

At inception, the Ministry of Niger Delta

Affairs had the mandate to coordinate efforts at ensuring infrastructural development, environmental protection and youth empowerment in the once-restive region. It promptly set out to satisfy the national clamor to remediate the region by embarking on numerous lofty projects all at once in a bid to fast track its mandate. These include road construction projects, prominent among them is the 337-kilometer East-West road traversing the Niger Delta Region which the ministry inherited from the ministry of works; various land reclamation and shoreline protection projects, building of skill acquisition centers across the oil producing states; various housing, water and rural electrification projects in communities spread across the region, among others.

Investigations by Sunday Vanguard, March 18, 2012 indicated that of a list of 311 itemized projects embarked upon between 2009 and 2011 which span across the ministry's mandate, 17 road projects some of which have 2013 completion dates are between 1.5 to 69.5 percent completion. It is sad to say that four years has gone by, none of the projects embarked upon by the ministry since its creation have been commissioned. In the area of skill acquisition, over 34,004 youths were shortlisted for training in ten identified sectors ranging from oil and gas to maritime, but only 701 youths were sent to India, Benin Republic and Israel to be trained in three out of ten sectors, namely – agriculture (90 youths), oil and gas (431 youths) and maritime (270 youths).

THE MINISTRY OF NIGER DELTA AFFAIRS

Most land reclamation, shoreline protection and canalization projects across the Niger Delta are still at consultancy stages with millions of Naira budgeted, construction of jetties, dredging and seaports development, as well as conservation and development of coastal ecosystems in seven states are yet to take off but was budgeted for. Despite these efforts and with over three years gone by the expectations of the people of Niger Delta and indeed, entire Nigerians keep growing just like the region's problems. Stakeholders have been irked that there has been no significant infrastructural facelift in the region. Besides, there has a sudden hull in project implementation by the ministry. One could be tempted to ask whether it is because of the bid to square up to its challenges that the ministry had bitten more than it can chew?

The ministry's yearly receipts from the federal government revealed that in 2009, out of a total of N96billion budgeted for the ministry the main and supplementary appropriations, a significant N94billion was released leaving a shortfall of N2billion. It turned out to be that this huge allocation in 2009 was like a bribe price for the ministry, so to say, as the story was not the same the following year. In 2010, out of a substantial appropriation of N145billion, the ministry received N58 billion leaving a whooping shortfall of N86.36billion. The deficit in releases of funds from the ministry of finance was repeated in 2011 as N35.6billion was released out of an approved budget of N52billion, forcing a shortfall of N16.3billion. In all, there was a cumulative shortfall of N104billion between 2009 to 2011, thus leaving projects already plunged into begging for progress and completion.

THE MINISTRY OF NIGER DELTA AFFAIRS

Aside the welcome achievement in youth training, stake-holders are bothered that as at today no single capital project is ready for commissioning despite the billions of naira allocated to the ministry year after year. Since its creation. However, as the ministry of Niger Delta Affairs - Elder Godsday Orubebe argued, this is not entirely the fault of the ministry. All the same, the ministry of Niger Delta Affairs certainly needs to up its ante if it wishes to avert a looming resurgence of militancy in the region.

11.1   Niger Delta Ministry Versus NDDC

As pointed out earlier, the creation of the ministry of Niger Delta Affairs tallies with the reasoning that all hands must be on deck to fast-track the development of the region that produces the oil-wealth of the nation. The ministry was supposed to lead and coordinate the infrastructural and environmental development as well as the youth empowerment programs of the federal government in the region. Those who supported the creation of the ministry were hopeful that it would attract additional funds and expertise for the rapid development of the region. A lot of premium was placed on the advantage of having two ministers who, as members of the federal executive council would have a platform to articulate the development needs of the Niger Delta. Those who were still not convinced were told that the Ministers would have easy access to Mr. President to ensure that he never loses sight of the Niger Delta question.

However, the story appears to be different more than three years after the creation of the Niger Delta's Ministry. The Ministry which many had thought was coming to add value to the fortunes of the region, is now confirming the worst fears of critics who predicted that it would slow down rather than enhance the activities of the Niger Delta Development Commission (NDDC) that it was supposed to complement. This is contrary to the general expectations that the ministry and the NDDC would team up to implement the Niger Delta Regional Development Master Plan. The unpleasant turn of events is, to say the least, shocking. Most people in the region had thought that a massive inflow of funds would follow the creation of the Ministry to translate the lofty goals of the Master Plan into projects and programs that would make significant impact on the lives of the people of the oil-bearing communities spread across the Niger Delta region.

In-fact, some people had suggested a Marshal plan approach in addressing the developmental challenges in the region.

It is rather sad indeed that this has not happened. To worsen matters, the ministry appears to be in a contest for superiority in its relationship with the NDDC. While other stakeholders are looking up to them to play a leading role in coordinating the implementation of the widely applauded master plan, the ministry seems intent on bringing NDDC under its control. The power tussle is uncalled for and the ministry should know that it was not put in place to reinvent the wheel. Basically, it was created to add more impetus to the activities of other agencies of government that are already on ground and partnering with them for the benefit of the region. Senator Ndoma-Egba, a strong voice in the upper legislative chamber of the National Assembly, puts it this way: "my understanding of the decision by the executive to create a ministry for the Niger Delta was to empower it to help in the infrastructural development of the area in addition to, not as a replacement for, what the NDDC is doing". Another law-maker in the House of Representatives – Hon. Daniel Regenieju, noted that the commission was established by an Act of Parliament – "On no account should the commission be merged with the ministry because the Niger Delta ministry was created by an executive fiat while the commission came to life via an Act of Parliament which is far stronger than that of the ministry" he asserted.

Again, the ministry should be aware that many Nigerians still believe that it is a superfluous political contraption. Recently, for instance, the former minister of the federal capital territory, Mallam Nasir El-Rufia said "the creation of the Niger Delta Ministry is a political gesture and unnecessary bureaucracy that will fail to solve the problem of the troubled region". Unfortunately, the ministry seems to be preoccupied with annexing more power and extending its spheres of influence, especially over other statutory agencies. The minister of Niger Delta Affairs, Elder Godsday Orubebe never hidden his disdain for an autonomous NDDC. He argued at every opportunity that the commission should be supervised by his ministry. In an interview published in a national newspaper, the minister said – there is no correlation between the NDDC and the Niger Delta ministry. If you go and attend a meeting anywhere in the world, people are talking to you about the NDDC, people are talking to you about the development and as a minister, you have little or no information about what the NDDC is doing, does that present any meaningful reasoning? A minister of the Niger Delta should be able to tell development partners and whoever that is concerned what is being done by the NDDC. But today, there is no correlation".

THE MINISTRY OF NIGER DELTA AFFAIRS

Indeed, the minister is right in insisting on collaboration between his ministry and the NDDC. But who or what are the hindrances to this very necessary partnership? Before the ministry was established, the NDDC had already set up a clearing house called the Partners for Sustainable Development (PSD) Forum. This important organ brings together representatives of federal and governments of oil-bearing states, youth and women leaders, traditional rulers as well as the organized private sector, civil society, the mass media and international development agencies such as the UNDP and the World Bank. It main function is to ensure that all the developmental activities in the Niger Delta by all stakeholders are synchronized. This important organ is all that the ministry needs to key into development programs of the region.

It is however surprising that the ministry has not adopted the master plan facilitated by the NDDC as its own road map, since the federal government gave its blessings for the production of the comprehensive plan. The 15year period of the plan must not be allowed to run out without any significant impact on the Niger Delta region. There is no room for distractive schism in what should be a collective effort to rescue Niger Deltans from the pits of Squalor and want. The Act setting up the NDDC clearly puts the supervision of the commission directly under the president; not under the presidency. This means that there are no obstructive go-between for the commission and the president to ensure expeditious implementation of the decisions. The framers of the law were conscious of the fact that the interventionist agency must be freed of all the encumbrances of ministries which are usually weighed down by bureaucratic red tape. Part II, Section 7 of the Niger Delta Development commission (Establishment) Act 2000 states that: "The commission shall be Subject to the direction, control or supervision in the performance of its functions under this Act by the President, commander-in-Chief of the Armed Forces of the Federal Republic of Nigeria".

THE MINISTRY OF NIGER DELTA AFFAIRS

The royal fathers in the region, under the aegis of Association of Traditional Rulers of oil mineral Producing communities of Nigeria (ATROMPCN) had given their wise counsel to President Goodluck Jonathan on this matter. Their warning: "Don't contemplate merging the commission with the ministry. Such action will be detriment al to the entire people of the area". The urgent task now is to secure more funds for the full implementation of the Master Plan for the region. There is indeed, enough room for both the ministry and the NDDC to operate and collaborate for the benefit of the Niger Deltans.

11.2   **Analysis of 2009, 2010, 2011, and 2012**

Budgets of the Ministry of Niger Delta Affairs

In 2009, a projected figure of N51billion was budgeted for the ministry of Niger Delta Affairs by the Federal Government. Out of this, local travels and transport was given N122.1 million, while international travel and transport was allocated N100million. In the same year, projected expenditure for local training was N98million. Security services and Allied matters N710million, Refreshment and meals N50million, security note (including operations) N35million, Niger Delta Coastal Road N300 million, peace and Security Employment corps N500million, amongst others. Importantly, lots one to four of the East West Road gulped N28billion in that fiscal year. Housing scheme and mortgage was N500 million.

For 2010 Federal Appropriation (Amended Act), the Niger Delta Ministry got an estimates of N86.2billion, with N205 million budgeted for travels and training N175 million for maintenance (general), N162.8 million for training (general), security and Allied matters N700million, Sea Boat Fuel N34million, Generator Fuel cost N25million, Refreshment and meals N30million, including meeting with youths and Elders N90 million. Further, New Town/ Industrial Park Development got N1.9Billion, with the cumulative lot of East West Road taking about N30billion in that fiscal year, amongst others.

THE MINISTRY OF NIGER DELTA AFFAIRS

In the 2011 Appropriation (Amended Act), a total of N55.2 Billion was allocated to the Ministry. From that amount, the ministry's overhead for the said year was put at N2.4 Billion, while Travels and Transport (general) was allocated N250million. Training (general) was allocated N1billion, which covered 'Non-militant Training Sensitization and mobilization', Security got N495 million. N41.5 Billion (blanket allocation for construction and provision for Roads – chat of account: 23020114). Refreshment and meals got N12million, Erosion and Flood Control (without spot in) N5.2Billion, Research and Development N100million with an allocation of N1billion as 'fund for Economic Empowerment, Training and post Training. There was also another N957 million as "fund for Economic Empowerment in 2010.

In the 2012 Budget Proposal of the Federal Government, the Niger Delta ministry is projecting to spend N59.7 billion. Out of this amount, over N449million is for travels and transport (including international travels and training, which is split into two subheads). Overhead expenditure of this ministry for 2012 is projected at N1.7billion. Further, maintenance of office furniture for 2012 is projected at N118.5 million. Expenditure for security services is projected at over N371 million, refreshment and meals N31.9 million.

Let me commend the effort of the budget office of the Federation for the improvement on the project site tracking and spot identity of projects in the 2012 Budget proposal by MDAs. In spite of that, it is unfortunate that there are still very unacceptable figures in the ministry's 2012 budget. Let us take for instance, the N4.2billion allocated for Research and development and another chat location figure of over N700 million for computer software acquisition, which should have been totally re-allocated to other matters in line with the procurement reality of fiscal discipline. One may like to ask: what was the N100 million allocated for Research and development used for in the 2011 Budget of the ministry? What is computer software that would cost about N800 million? Curiously, there is another N547 million for ICT Networking centers and connectivity for the offices of the ministry in the nine states of the Niger Delta. Meaning that, over a Billion Naira would be used for ICT and computers by the ministry in 2012. Again, one is tempted to ask, if the ministry doesn't already have internet access, how come N20 million was allocated for internet access charge by the ministry in 2009? What also did the ministry spend the N431 million for ICT connectivity centre for its 2010 Budget? This amount to fiscal indiscipline and an assault on the suffering people of the Niger Delta. However, there are other questionable allocations to be discussed later.

THE MINISTRY OF NIGER DELTA AFFAIRS

Be-
tween 2009 and 2011, about N92 million in aggregate had been allocated to feeding alone within this ministry. If the projected estimate of N31.9 million for feeding and refreshment as captured in 2012 Budget is given a legislative bite, then the ministry alone would be spending over N150 million for Feeding and Refreshment within a period of four years, when over a million people or more cannot afford a square meal daily in the Niger Delta the ministry was created to develop. There is also about a Billion Naira expended by the ministry on Training from 2009 to 2011, which is also outside the N1 Billion for non-militant Training and Sensitization. These figures are enough at training hundreds of our young people in the Niger Delta and with additional incentives like revolving (monetary) grants for capacity stabilization. It is only the ministry of Niger Delta that can explain what derivable gains these figures have added to human capital development within the Niger Delta. There was another N1 Billion as 'Fund for Economic Development', which was allocated in 2011. Therefore, if the N449 million further allocated for training in the 2012 budget is allowed to go, then, closed to about N3 Billion would be expended by this ministry at the end of 2012 Budget circle on training alone.

THE MINISTRY OF NIGER DELTA AFFAIRS

At a time when defense budget is taking a huge chunk of the nation's budgeting provision, it is sad and totally unacceptable to see government ministries competing with the security agencies for security line-budgets that are directly expended by these MDAs themselves. Between 2009 and 2011, the ministry had appropriated a total of N2.4 Billion for security alone. If the N371 million projected for 2012 is added, close to N3 Billion shall be expended on security. At the same time, the state government, local government, oil companies, military formation(s) (JTF) spent additional sums daily on security. The N3 Billion here described is outside another hundreds of Millions budgeted by the ministry for oil and gas asset Protection Program, which is still under security but given another name and budget heading. These huge funds can do for an entire year budget of some local government areas in the Niger Delta.

At this juncture, the question begging for answer is: why is the federal government and the Niger Delta Ministry spending Billions on security in a region where government is spending so much on amnesty program? Is this huge security expenditure for crime suppression, economic exploitation or for provision of stable social environment and peace? What also did the ministry spend the N50million it allocated for study, design and technology centre on in 2009? Niger Delta People are interested to know where the technology centre is located within the region.

It is commendable to see that the ministry's expenditure on 'Generator Fuel cost' is reducing from N32 million in 2009, N25 million in 2010 to about N5 million in 2011. But how economically wise for separate ministries to be maintaining their own generators in the federal secretariat that is supposed to be centrally powered? Let us now take a look at the ministry's capital projects for 2012. Built in the 2012 capital expenditure of the Ministry is the Idoro Eastern Itam Water Projects for N400 million. There was already a N50 million allocated for this same project in 2011. what was the N50 million allocated in 2011 used for?

The Owerri Urban Water Scheme is another fiscal setback. In 2010, the project was allocated N292.5 million. In 2011, another N50 million was allocated and again another N500 million is projected for this project in 2012. This shows that from 2010 to the 2012 fiscal year, over N842 million is projected for this single project at Owerri Urban. Other water projects include the Ubane Utanga water Project in Cross River state, which was allocated N50million in 2011 with another N516 million projected for the same project in the 2012 budget. That brings it to a total of about N911 million within four years. Where are the huge sums previously allocated to this project?

THE MINISTRY OF NIGER DELTA AFFAIRS

This is equally applicable to Ukparam water project in Ondo state. That project got N100 million in 2009, N97 million in 2010,and N150 million in 2011, with another N177 million projected for in 2012. Cummulatively, in four years, this project could gulp N424 million. Moreover, Niger Deltans are curious to know which community (Isiokpo?) in Ikwere local government benefited from the N195 million (2010) and another N50 million in (2011) and (Ibaa?) in Rivers state 2011. It is sad that a community like Alesa in Eleme local government has suffered rolling and duplicitous allocations of huge sums for project(s) the people never saw, or heard of. To put record straight the ministry should endeavour to pin-point the exact location any project, the clan and local government where such projects are located. The allocation of N100 million by the ministry of Niger Delta in 2011 for (Eleme?) water project without any clear location is indeed, questionable.

The Niger Delta Development Commission (NDDC) budgeted N244 million for a major 'Water Works' in Ales clan, out of which N36.6 million had been committed to the contractor and with a Budget of N48.8 million approved as part of this in 2011 NDDC Budget. This is a contradiction, considering the fact that, Niger Delta Basin and Rural

Development Authority (NDBRDA) has (claimed to) to be spending tens of millions of Nair for the same Alesa Water Project since 2006. Why suffocate the local people this way: same Alesa community was given a Budget line of N50 million in 2011 for land Reclamation in a community that is not riverine. This same ministry earlier had allocated N50 million each for shoreline protection and canalization of Aleto and Ekporo communities in Eleme local government in 2011. Shockingly, these communities are upland with fairly good soil topography. Can the ministry of Niger Delta Affairs and NDDC intentionally allocate figures to projects, which an Agency like Niger Delta Basin and Rural Development Authority had also claimed intervention on? Is this duplication due to absence of inter-agencies intelligence and synergy? If the (MDAs) have held Budget Town Hall meetings within the region, they could have known the truth of the situation.

THE MINISTRY OF NIGER DELTA AFFAIRS

On Electricity, a project for Khana local government area of Rivers State was allocated N200 million in 2009, N263.2 million in 2010, N50 million in 2011 with another N200 million projected in the 2012 budget which would bring it to over half a billion Naira (that is, over N700 million) within the period. This should interest the people of Khana and the local government Authority there. Erei Electrification Project in Cross River state was allocated N100 million in 2009, N97 million in 2010, and N50 million in 2011 with another N200 million allocated to same project in 2012. for the Peremabiri-ogbokiri Electrification project in Bayelsa State, N200 million was allocated in 2009, N195 million in 2010, N50 million in 2011 with another N400 million in 2012. This adds up to a total single expenditure projection of N845 million by 2012.

As at 2009, several billion was allocated to skill acquisition centres by the ministry as chain-figures. In 2009, N2.7 billion was allocated as a line item. There was also another allocation of N200 million for a skill acquisition centre in Akoko-Edo in Edo state. N127 million Mosogar skill Acquisition centre, N200 million for Oguta, in Imo state, and N300 million for Ikwere in Rivers State, N800 million for Technology centre in Eleme local government Area, excluding design and prototype which was allocated N50 million that year. In 2010, a lumped sum of N8.7 billion for the same skill Acquisition Centre was proposed. By 2011, another N2.5 billion was allocated for the same set of skill Acquisition projects; with N5 billion also projected for the same project in 2012. Cumulatively, about N11 billion would be expended on this set of projects.

THE MINISTRY OF NIGER DELTA AFFAIRS

On road construction, the 21.9 kilometres

Ekparakwa-Ukanafun-Ikot Udo-Aba Road was allocated N500 million in 2009, N975 million in 2010, N10 million in 2011 while N900 million was projected for the same road in 2012. Still on Roads, Omelema-Agada Road in Rivers state was allocated N100 million in 2009, N975 million for same in 2012 budget. One can go on and on and mention so many Roads Projects that have appeared and re-appeared in the ministry's budgets from 2009 till date. The point is, where is the money going? If these figures are actually used for capital projects within the region, there could have been massive construction projects going on at the same time in the Region.

Finally, a comprehensive desk review of NDDC, ministry of Niger Delta Affairs (MNDA), States and local governments Budgets within the Niger Delta could reveal a catalogue of wastage and fraud. Reasonable time is devoted to present this exposition because it is believed that there is need to radically define the way government budgets are formulated and applied. However, its suggested here that the Budget office of the Federation (BOF) and the Bureau of public procurement (BPP) to put in place a mandatory requirement, which compels MDAs to present a community-centred and endorsed needs Assessment Reports for all new capital (construction) Projects. Such should be accompanied by the minutes of community Budget Town Hall meetings endorsed by representatives of communities, with the documents to accompany request for approval for MDAs procurement plans to the BPP, such community representatives(s) also should endorse satisfactory project completion memos of communities which shall be attached as addendum, with request for issuance of job completion certificates and final payment.

CHAPTER TWELVE

NIGER DELTA AMNESTY: IN PERSPECTIVE

It is undisputable fact that the cause of the crisis in the oil region is the lack of human capabilities which are fundamental for one to have a decent and dignifies life. Such capabilities lacking in the region include shelter, food education, employment, security etc. The Ogoni Bill of Rights written by the MOSOP (Movement for the Survival of Ogoni People), one of the earliest and most organized non-violent social movement in the Niger Delta, concisely and succinctly present these human capabilities lacking in the region in the following way:

> *That the search for oil has caused severe land and food shortages in Ogoni, one of the most densely populated areas in Africa... that neglectful of the environmental pollution laws and substandard inspection techniques of the federal authorities have led to the complete degradation of the Ogoni environment, turning our homeland into an ecological disaster ... that the Ogoni lack education, health and other social facilities ... that it is intolerable that one of richest areas of Nigeria should wallow in abject poverty and destitution ... that the Ogoni people wish to manage their own affairs.*

It is the lack of these capabilities which are fundamental for human functioning that Nussbaum in her theory of capabilities, regards as both unjust and tragic because the people are systematically falling below the threshold in core areas of human capabilities and, as such calls it capabilities failure. According to her, such situation calls for an urgent attention. Nigerian government in its effort to resolve the crisis in oil region proposed an amnesty policy targeted at the militants who were to lay down their arms. However, since the cause of the Niger Delta crisis is capabilities failure and the demands of the Niger Delta people right from the days the social movements were non-violent to the time it became violent, has always been improved human capabilities, it can safely be inferred that addressing the issue of capabilities failure which has always been the aspirations of the people will bring about a genuine and desire peace in the region. The question then is what is the possibility of the amnesty policy addressing the issue of capabilities failure in the long troubled region and to what extent? Answers to these questions would be provided after appraisal of the factors which informed the federal government declaration of amnesty to the Niger Delta militants.

NIGER DELTA AMNESTY: IN PERSPECTIVE

14.1. **The Loses**

A major impetus for the Amnesty program

was the devastating impacts of the crisis occasioned by the activities of militant groups which at its peak, reportedly cost the nation about N8.7 billion daily while production slumped from 2.3 million barrels per day to just about a million barrels. This was aside the incalculable human and environmental casualties and damages inflicted on the nation.

According to Timi Alaibe, erstwhile Presidential Adviser on Niger Delta, by January 2009, militancy in the Niger Delta had virtually crippled Nigeria's economy. Investment inflow to the upstream sub-sector of the oil industry had dwindled remarkably. Exasperated foreign investors had begun redirecting their investments to Angola and Ghana preferred destinations over Nigeria. At that point, Angola surpassed Nigeria as Africa's highest crude oil producer. This dwindling investments in the critical oil and gas sectors threatened Nigeria's capacity to grow its crude oil reserves as planned. Clearly, insecurity in the Niger Delta was identified as key reason why investors were leaving for more stable business opportunities in Africa. For example, due to militant activities in the Niger Delta, Royal Dutch Shell by early 2009, saw its production drop from one million barrels per day to about 250, 000 barrels per day. ExxonMobil also experienced increased insurgent activity in its Nigerian operations Sabotage, oil siphoning rackets and kidnapping of oil workers by suspected militants further threatened the operations of the oil companies and exerted immense pressure on the Nigerian economy. Worse still, citing insecurity, union officials all too often called strikes to protest unsecured working environment.

NIGER DELTA AMNESTY: IN PERSPECTIVE

However, the situation got to a point where Nigeria's export dwindled to as low as 800,000 bpd, compared with a targeted 2.2 million bpd for the first quarter of 2009. In 2008 alone, it was estimated that Nigeria lost over 3trillion Naira as a result of militancy in the Niger Delta. Huge as the financial loss might sound, the human loss occasioned by the Niger Delta crisis is mind boggling, as typified by what later came to be referred to as "the Odi Massacre". To shade more lights on Odi's carnage, the Ugly incidence began in early November 1999,when a group of lawless elements abducted six police officers in Odi, Bayelsa state. And despite the intervention of social movements in the Niger Delta and elsewhere in the country as well as the Bayelsa state government officials, the law officers were killed by the hoodlums. The then president-Obasanjo O. issued a 14-day Ultimatum to Bayelsa state government to produce the miscreants, failing which he will proclaim a state of emergency.

With no result forthcoming, the president ordered troops into Odi and a Major Military Operation commenced, via the use of heavy artillery, aircraft, grenade launchers, mortar bombs and other sophisticated weapons. According to Abdul Oroh, Executive Director, Civil Liberty Organization, Nigeria, the invasion was code named "operation Hakuri II" by the then Minister of Defense-General T.Y. Danjuma. Briefing the ministerial conference on November 25, explained operation Hakuri II on Odi and other communities of the Niger Delta thus:

> *"This operation Hakuri II was initiated with the mandate of protecting lives and property-particularly oil platforms flow stations, operating rig terminals and pipelines, refineries and power installation in the Niger Delta".*

NIGER DELTA AMNESTY: IN PERSPECTIVE

The casualty figure of the invasion remains unknown but some reports however puts it at about 2, 000 lives, while others contest it as being lower than the actual figures.

14.2.   **The Amnesty**

The vision statement of the Amnesty Program is to create "A Niger Delta Region populated with modern cities with leading edge environmental management practices, economic prosperity, skilled and healthy people and social harmony. The terms of the Amnesty included the willingness and readiness of militants to surrender their arms, unconditionally, renounce militancy and sign an undertaking to this effect. In return, government pledged its commitment to institute programs to assist their disarmament, demobilization, rehabilitation and provision of reintegration assistance to the militants. These were Major preconditions to address wider development challenges in the Niger Delta. The acceptance of the offer of amnesty by the repentant militants was also predicated on the promise by government that the ex-militants would be reformed and reintegrated into civil society. The federal government also stated its determination to confront head-on the neglect and sundry development challenges that had bred the insecurity and militancy in the Niger Delta.

14.3.   Counting The Gains Of Amnesty Program

Despite some criticisms of the amnesty program of the federal government, certain gains have so far been recorded. In discussing the fruits of amnesty program, most people point at the primacy of economic benefits of increased oil production and relative peace in the Niger Delta. However, there are other intangible benefits that far outweigh the economic boom heralded by the Amnesty program. The transformational activities offered by ex-agitators that resort to violence is more powerful than nonviolence. Ex-combatants have been relieved of the burden of violence and now, the youth have been given the opportunity of career guidance to realize their aspirations in terms of education, vocational and entrepreneurial skills.

NIGER DELTA AMNESTY: IN PERSPECTIVE

With relative peace restored in the Niger Delta, oil companies and associated companies re-opened shut-in wells. The result is that Nigeria's oil production increased from 800, 000 barrels per day to 2.7 million barrels per day. With cessation of hostilities, government has assured the international community of filling its OPEC quota and be trusted by major consumer nations to meet its contractual obligations. Oil bunkering reduced, signs that the process would succeed and accelerate economic development across the nation with renewed confidence in the international oil market, Nigeria has started to exercise enormous influence in OPEC. The increase in Nigeria's quota of oil production is a result of reduced incidence of Kidnapping, which provides the right environment for the repairs of oil and gas infrastructures damaged during the period of militant agitation. It has also provided ample opportunity for contractors handling development in the Niger Delta.

Addressing newsmen in a press conference in Abuja on February 2012, the chairman of the Presidential Amnesty Program, Hon. Kingsley Kuku, outlined the benefits of the amnesty program to include: entrenching peace in the creeks, drastically reducing the menace of kidnapping, destruction oil facilities and increase in the nation's quota of oil production. He attributed the success achieved in the program to the determination of President Goodluck Jonathan to sustain peace and security of live and property in the country, while at the same time creating conducive environment for oil production and foreign direct investment. The Presidential Amnesty Program (PAP) boss made it clear that the program has accommodated more than 26,000 youths from the Niger Delta Region, adding that although some youths vehemently advocating for inclusion, the program has closed. According to him, only a proclamation by Mr. President can open a new phase of the amnesty program.

14.4.   Criticism of the Amnesty

However, the amnesty program has come under heavy criticism both in terms of structural deficiency and operational ambiguity. Kathryn Nwajiaku-Dahou of the Sub-saharan Africa Program insists that the announcement of the amnesty package spear-headed a rush to acquire "militancy" status and a rush to hand in weapons of any kind by would-be beneficiaries, throughout the Niger Delta states and beyond. This was equally the case in states where oil production was minimal and in which there had been little recorded recent history of militant activity, even though the kidnapping phenomenon had become widespread. The lack of clarity about how inclusion was to be determined, i.e., who could be eligible for stipends and rehabilitation training and the amounts involved also created confusion and much discontent between would-be 'legitimate' militants and 'so called militants' who were also reaping benefits.

NIGER DELTA AMNESTY: IN PERSPECTIVE

Furthermore, David Smock of the United States Institute of Peace believes that the existing process in the Niger Delta made no carefully planned provision for reintegration which should include resettlement, training, alternative employment, etc. One potential resource that has remained untapped is the preparedness of some oil companies to assist with technical training to enhance the employment of those given amnesty. Second, as with most DDR programs around, the world, probably only a fraction of existing weapons were being surrendered and it is not even clear that the weapons being turned in were those used by the militants. Third, for a DDR process to be fully successful, it needs to be part of a comprehensive peace process. Without addressing the grievances of the militants and others in the Delta, it is unlikely that DDR can succeed. Fourth, many militants would have greater confidence in the disarmament process if international monitors were invited as witnesses with assurance that the weapons turned in are put beyond use. But the government had resisted international observers. Fifth, some militants understand the purpose of the amnesty process to be a means of dividing the militants against each other.

On the other hand, the operational ambiguity of the program is reflected in the absence of a definite time-frame for post-amnesty rehabilitation process. This has been described by observers as possibly, a means to cover up the misuse of public funds. They insist that despite the laudable gains attributed to the post amnesty program – like increased crude oil production and decline in militant related violence and kidnapping in the region, no one in government seems to know what exactly comes next, hence the open-endedness of the programme. The projects, particularly those requiring much public funds, should have a defined time frame for their execution in order to ensure that their pursuit is not hijacked and used as a means to Siphon public funds. But the former special adviser to the committee, Timi Alaibe, is documented as describing the final stage of the post-amnesty programme- reintegration – as essentially a social and economic process with an open time-frame.

NIGER DELTA AMNESTY: IN PERSPECTIVE

Hence, the exact figures regarding how many are involved in the scheme and how much each individual is getting remains muddled. It is reported that weekly stipend of N21, 000 is paid to each of the ex-militant on the scheme. And it is note-worthy that this approximation does not take into account the figures spent on hotel accommodation and training, among other costs. The exact number of ex-militants involved in the programme fluctuates between 20,000 and 26,000. And it is currently unknown how much is required to maintain the programme each year. Last year-2011, saw budgetary estimates balloon from an initial N58 billion to N65 billion.

To address the earlier question posed with regards to the possibility of the amnesty policy addressing the issue of capabilities failure in the Niger Delta, it has been noted that the amnesty policy is focused only on the militants as was announced by the late President Yar'Adua. Hence, the emphasis of the presidential implementation committee on disarmament, rehabilitation and reintegration of the militants in the Nigerian Society. And what prompted the proposal of the policy was because the militancy in the region has severe adverse effect on the oil industry which is the economic life wire of the country as an oil state. The militancy reduced the production capacity of the oil sector to less than half, making Angola, as pointed out earlier, the second highest oil producing nation in Africa to become first. This implies that the policy aims only at stopping the violent conflict against the state and the oil companies to ensure the continuous flow of oil.

In the same vein, Kenneth Omeje argues that

NIGER DELTA AMNESTY: IN PERSPECTIVE

"the prime concern of the Nigerian state in the management of conflict in the Niger Delta has been to maximize the oil revenues" (Omeje 2004:425). As the policy literally made no mention of plans of addressing the lacking capabilities in the oil region, it has no potentiality on improving the human capabilities of the people of the region. Indeed, the interest and end which prompted the Nigerian government to intervene in Niger Delta crisis is the oil revenue. It has always been its interest and end in any conflict management strategy in the region. There was nothing about addressing the demands and aspirations of the people in the region in the policy which would have warranted treating them as ends and as such ensure that they get the basic entitlements necessary for human functioning and flourishing. And Nussbaum while quoting Karl Marx, notes that it is wrong to sub-ordinate the ends of some individuals to those of others because that is the core of what exploitation is to treat a person as mere object for the use of others. (Nussbaum 2008: 73).

It is a truism that Dr. Tmiebi Koripamo-Agary, a member of the presidential Amnesty Implementation Committee argues that there cannot be development without peace. While Korpano-Agary's argument seems plausible since there has been violence militancy in the region for some time, it should be noted however, that capabilities failure in the region is an issue that has lasted for half a century that the oil was discovered in the region. And none of the successive Nigerian government has ever made any significant attempt to address it. And even more than two years after the policy was proposed and implemented, with the seeming compliance, except a faction of MEND, of the militants in the region which brought relative peace, the capabilities state in the Niger Delta region is still the same with no plan by the government, either proximate or remote one, to address the situation.

It was as a result of this persistent indifference of the Nigerian government to address the root cause of the crises that many people in the region entertain fears that there may be a resurgence and of course, there was with the attack and destruction of Agip trunk line at Brass by MEND in February 2012. In this regard, Sabella Ogbobode Abidde, an activist from the oil region notes that "with respect to the amnesty – it may blow up because there are no proper and genuine attempts at post-conflict reconstruction. There are no plans underway to tackle the cause of the agitation". Such a fear was reasonable as event turned out to show, and because the amnesty policy of the federal government which has no proper and genuine post conflict plans but only aims at disarming, rehabilitating and reintegrating the militants, can be likened to one treating symptoms of a disease while the disease persist. Such a disease must eventually resurface and may be in a worse form because it is still untreated. And so will the Niger Delta crisis if the real issue in the crisis, which is capabilities failure, is not urgently addressed. From the foregoing, it can be gathered that the issue of capabilities failure in the Niger Delta and it appears that the policy was either programmed to fail, ab-initio, or, perhaps, was hijacked and transmuted into a fat cow by those who were entrusted with the responsibility of overseeing the transformation of the ex-militants into law abiding citizens of Nigeria. The next chapter shall look into proposal for post-amnesty programme in the Niger Delta.

NIGER DELTA AMNESTY: IN PERSPECTIVE

CHAPTER THIRTEEN

PROPOSAL FOR POST-AMNESTY PROGRAMME

This chapter shall attempt a proposal for a course of action that the Federal government of Nigeria can take in order to consolidate the gains of amnesty programme by building peace and engineering people-centred development in the Niger Delta. This proposal intends to use the institutional analysis and Development (IAD) framework to diagnose the missing to addressing the crisis in the Niger Delta. While the amnesty policy has yielded some positive results in that most of the militant groups had embraced the policy and are undergoing same training(s) both within and outside Nigeria, the grey area-post-amnesty plan – that can address the problems and challenges that triggered violence, insecurity and economic loss in the region requires urgent attentions. In other words, amnesty programme needs be complemented with pragmatic post-amnesty poverty reduction and development strategies that are people-oriented. It is appropriate to make hay while the sun shines. This proposal designs a Niger Delta post-amnesty development model (NDPADM) that derives inspirations and workability mechanisms from fifteen (15) African development models that are problem-solving and solution-seeking in several sectors of the economy in the Niger Delta.

13.1 Niger Delta Post-Amnesty Development Model (NDPADM)

Niger Delta post-Amnesty Development model is conceptualized as a deliberate act of combining both the 'known' and the 'unknown' variables in the Niger Delta using the institutional Analysis and Development (IAD) framework and several pragmatic problem-solving and solution-seeking African Development models (see Figure 1). Niger Delta post-amnesty development model (NDPADM) derives inspirations and working mechanism from fifteen (15) African development models (Akinola

PROPOSAL FOR POST-AMNESTY PROGRAMME

2007,   g.i;
2008f, m, p; 2010a, b). the 15 models are: (1) African intellectual gap measurement model (AGIMM) for measuring intellectual potentials and relevance of African universities as well as intellectual gap(s) among African Scholars with the aim of reforming African educational curriculum and making African scholarship problem-solving and solution-seeking (see Akinola 2008m for details on this model); (2) African public sphere restructuring model (APSRM) for the setting up self-governing community assembly (SGCA) for deliberation, collegiality, mutual trust, reciprocity to enable citizens, both elite and non-elite to operate in synergy to collectively achieve socio-economic and techno-political objective (for details, see Akinola

2010a, b). (3) African Development Institutional Mechanism (ADIM) for connecting all the stakeholders in development at various levels of decision making (Akinola: 2007f); (4) African Polycentric Information Networking (APIN) for creating networks between the leaders and the people for effective information sharing and communication (Akinola 2008p: 188-189); (5) African Food security model (AFSM) for securing food for the citizens (Akinola 2008f, p.193-195); (6) African Employment Generation Model (AGEM) for generating employment opportunities (Akinola 2008p: 193-195); (7) African conflict Prevention and peace Building (ACPPB) for detecting and preventing conflict as well as building peace (Akinola 2008p:189); (8) African sustainable Environment model (ASEM) for conserving and protecting environmental resources (Akinola 2008q); (9) African Road Triology (ART) for building cost effective and durable roads (Akinola 1998); (10) African community-initiative and Development model (ACID) for empowering the people economically and reducing poverty (Akinola 2000: 186-187); (11) African Electoral Reform and Democratization (AERD) for inclusive democratization (Akinola 2008p: 192-193); (12) African Local Economic Development Strategy (ALEDS) fro enhancing economic growth through local industrialization and sustaining development (Akinola 2007: 233; 2008f, p: 190-191); (13) African Polycentric Privatization model (APPM) for distributing the benefits of economic growth among the citizenry (Akinola 2007f: 233); (14) African Polycentric Security Model (APSM) for ensuring security of lives and property (Akinola 2009a: 270-271); and (15) African Human Resources Development and Utilization Model (AHRDUM) for bridging the gaps between developers and utilizers of human resources.

PROPOSAL FOR POST-AMNESTY PROGRAMME

Niger Delta Post-Amnesty Development Model (ND-PADM) is diagrammatized in *figure Ia*. According to the diagram, the known variables are: the number of 'amnested' persons, budget earmarked for amnesty programme, training and job opportunities. Assuming that the amnesty works by making life better for the disarmed militants, will that not be creating a pathway for jobless youths to go into militancy so that they can also be taken care of through future amnesty programmes? Will some 'amnested' individuals whose lives are made better not be tutoring other youth on how to go through the process of "violence-amnesty-better life"? These are some of the questions that demand critical reflections. Without a restructuring that could enable all the diverse interests in the Niger Delta to operate as colleagues with equal standing such that oil benefits are shared equitably, amnesty programme will amount to fire brigade exercise and a waste of resources. In order to avoid this scenario, this proposal is paying attention to post-amnesty plan and strategies to enable the gains of the amnesty programme to be properly consolidated.

PROPOSAL FOR POST-AMNESTY PROGRAMME

Fig. 1:
Niger Delta Post-Amnesty Development
Model (NDPADM)

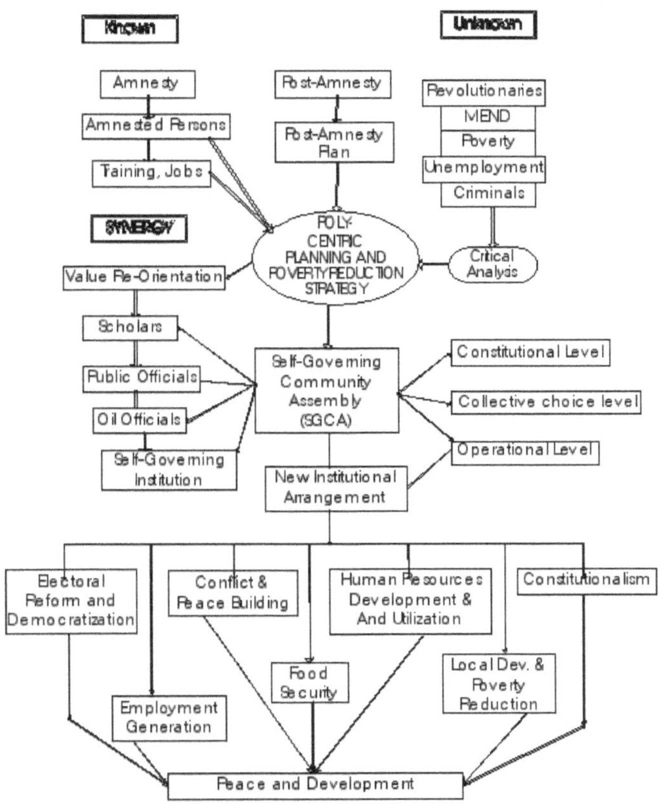

Source: *Adapted from Akinola (2007f, 2010 a,b)*

PROPOSAL FOR POST-AMNESTY PROGRAMME

On the other hand (fig.1), unknown variables include: the number and likely impact of revolutionaries, the reconstruction of MEND, the dynamics of poverty and neglect, unemployment, participants within action arenas in response to their particular exogenous variables. This normally starts when participants within an action arena respond to exogenous variable or context (biophysical/material conditions, cultural and other attributes of a community, and rules-in-use) and when outcomes are positive the participants will increase their commitment to maintain the structure as it is or to another set of exogenous variables and then on and on like that. However, if outcomes are negative, participants might raise some questions on why the outcome are negative. They might then move to a different level and change their institutions to produce another set of interactions and consequently, differently outcomes. Thus, the model believes that the fifteen models (mentioned earlier) can work in the Niger Delta if conditions for collective action are fulfilled.

The conditions for collective action can be fulfilled when deliberate action is taken to set up a new institutional arrangement through polycentric planning and poverty reduction strategy (PPPRS) whereby the efforts of the stakeholders/participants in the public terrains – politicians, bureaucrats, technocrats, scholars, multinationals and citizens – are synergized through public sphere restructuring mechanism (see details, Akinola 2012a,b). The restructuring process will commence, first, with the setting up of self-governing community assembly (SGCA) where participants through their institutions (government with their agencies, oil companies, higher institutions, community institutions) can operate in synergy. The second step is a value re-orientation among African scholars, public officials and other participants. This new orientation, invariably, determines: (a) the ability of African scholars to take theories to the streets and applied them for the benefit of the citizenry (b) the synergy between and among African scholars and public officials in executing socio-economic and techno-political projects; (c) the relevance and indispensability of community self-governing institutions in decision making; and (d) the centrality and imperativeness of community assembly for decision making and resolution of crisis.

PROPOSAL FOR POST-AMNESTY PROGRAMME

Next, the participants would operate using rules that are crafted by members at the SGCA. Rule crafting takes place at three levels – constitutional, collective choice and operational. At the constitutional level lies the system that determines how rules are made and can be modified. At the heart of effective governance of Niger Delta is the imperativeness of constitutional reform (Akinola 2006, e) which can be accomplished through pragmatic experience, for example, polycentric privatization and local industrialization. The effectiveness of this strategy has been proved in an experiment performed in Irepodun local government area of Osun state, Nigeria between 2005 and 2006 by Akinola (2007f:230). Based on the Irepodun experience, the adoption of polycentric privatization strategy could avail the citizens in the Niger Delta the opportunities to dialogue in community assembly and jointly take decision on how resources (financial and natural) are to be allocated and utilized. At the collective choice level, rules that define and constrain the actions of individuals and citizens have to be established. At the operational level, concrete actions have to be undertaken by these individuals most directly affected, or by public officials (McGinnis 1999a).

This is where amnesty programme of the Federal government becomes relevant: 'Amnested' persons should be involved in the activities of community assembly where they can function as agent of change in development arenas. The experience of Saki initiatives in Oke-Ogun, Ogo state, Nigeria in transforming members of Oodua Peoples' Congress (OPC) from violent orientation to positive result such that there exists a symbiotic relationship between OPC and the local government towards community security is instructive (Akinola 2009a: 270-271). Invariably, the amnesty programme of the federal government would enable ex-militants freedom fighters and revolutionists to make meaningful contributions towards development. The self-governing institutions can act as checks and balances on the local government officials.

The outcome of restructuring is emergence of a new institutional arrangements, which would reflect integrative constitutional order in socio-economic and techno-political realms. It is this joint action and synergy by the three groups (scholars, public official and representatives of community self-governing institutions) that would eventually determine how government policies in all spheres of life are to be implemented. After the institutional arrangement has been designed, operational strategy for implementation of any programmed / project (e.g employment generation, food security, road development, poverty reduction, environmental management, electoral reform and democratization, security of life and property, conflict detection, prevention and resolution, etc) can then be fashioned out(Akinola 2007f; 2008b, 2009a, ;f, 2010a, b). It is at this stage that any of the fifteen models can be applied to any of the specific action situations. The result of post-amnesty polycentric development planning as shown in fig.1 and 1b is peace and people-centred development.

PROPOSAL FOR POST-AMNESTY PROGRAMME

Fig 1b (Continuation of fig.1): **Niger Delta Post Amnesty Development Model**

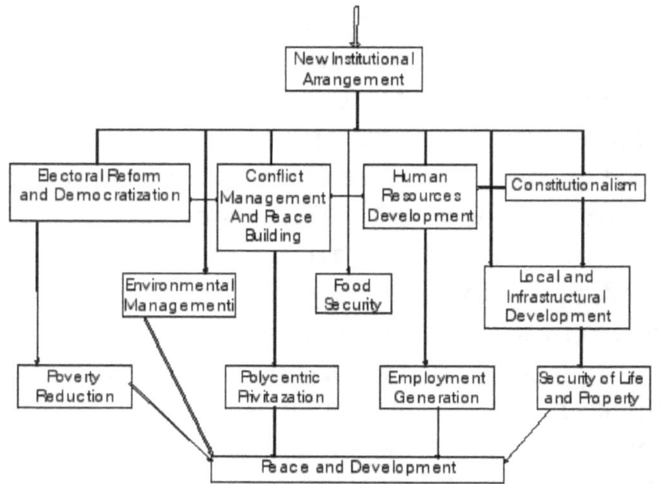

Source: *Adapted from Akinola (2007f, 2010 a, b).*

PROPOSAL FOR POST-AMNESTY PROGRAMME

13.2　Models in Brief

The fifteen models that would help in actualizing restructuring in the Niger Delta are discussed briefly below:

1.　African Intellectual Gap Measurement Model (AIGMM)

It is obvious that the institutional mechanism and technical know-how to take theories to the streets in Africa have not been adequately explored, hence, the persistent gap between theories and realities in the continent. It is in the light of this exigency that African Intellectual gap measurement model (AIGMM) is designed to measure intellectual potentials and relevance of African Universities and other higher educational Institutions in Africa (Akinoa 2008 m). The starting point is to determine what is missing in African scholarship by measuring intellectual gaps. The result of the measurement would determine the type of models that need to be designed to fill the identified gap(s). It is then imperative to test the models and refine them to ensure they fit into realities and become problem-solving. Knowledge management tools and techniques as well as effective planning and institutional framework that can make knowledge generated by African scholars relevant to the needs and aspirations of the People of the Niger Delta would need to be employed. Such home-grown development models developed by African scholars would need to be applied on pilot scale so that findings and experiences generated from these pilot cases would help in refining and modifying the models for full replication across the Niger Delta. The findings and experiences gathered from these exercises would invariably, be part of what could be used to reform African educational curriculum at university level (Akinola 2008m for details).

2. **African Public Sphere Restructuring Model (APSRM)**

African Public Sphere Restructuring Model (APSRM) is conceptualized as a deliberate act of setting up self-governing community assembly (SGCA) for deliberation, collegiality, mutual trust, reciprocity and shared community of understanding (Akinola 2010a, b). The models contends that, since political factor determines the operation of other sectors of economy, the starting point is to commence with application of strategies that can restructure the public sphere in the Niger Delta so that socio-economic and technological crisis in the region can be addressed on pilot scales. The model addresses reconstruction and reconfiguration of the public sphere in the Niger Delta to synergize the efforts of the people through their institutions and that of governments to resolve the lingering socio-economic crises and poverty in the region. At the same time, it charts a course of action on how citizens at community level can be mainstreamed in decision making, rule-monitoring and enforcement of sanction on rule infraction. APSRM emphasizes two-deliberation and deliberateness / action. It derives inspirations and working mechanisms from twelve(12) African development models (Akinola 2007f, 2008f, M,p).

PROPOSAL FOR POST-AMNESTY PROGRAMME

3. African Development Institutional Mechanism (ADIM)

African Development Institutional Mechanism (ADIM) could be applied to enable primary development players (scholars and public officials) in the Niger Delta to operate in synergy at regional and state levels. Applying ADIM to the Niger Delta, scholars should view the Niger Delta realities with intellectual lenses through exogenous variables by factoring exogenous variables into their study and understanding of the Niger Delta realities; otherwise, such studies will be repeating the error to the past-illusion. Scholars should generate knowledge through relevant applied research and analysis of existing scholarship focused on over-coming the Niger Delta's problems. Then scholars should pass knowledge on to the political sector(public officials). And public official, along with scholars, should implement policies (Akinola 2007f).

4. **African Polycentric Information Networking System (APIN)**

African polycentric Information Networking system (APIN) could be applied to strengthen linkages and interactions between individuals and self-governing institutions (Akinola 2008p: 188-189). The beauty of polycentricity is in its multifarious connections and interactive links that all members of a particular community have to receive information, interact and make contributions to receive information, interact and make contributions to decision making and conflict resolution: For example, decision taken or information passed in a polycentric system has the possibility of reaching every member of a community through at least four of eight channels. Each of the eight associations (occupation, religion, neighbourhood, cooperatives, women, youth, unemployed, and ethnic militia) is a channel for information dissemination. Since these institutions naturally draw their members without much difficulty, the linkages and interactions can then be connected to the state structure of governance. The networks once established can be useful at various domains of human interactions in the Niger Delta, from regional to state and then to local/community levels.

5. **African Conflict Prevention and Peace Building (ACPPB)**

African conflict Prevention and Peace Building (ACPPB) is designed to detect, prevent and resolve conflict, from national to local/community levels. It is believed that since members are from all associations that cut across the whole community, any action, information or rumor that may engender conflict would be detected earlier and necessary mechanisms at preventing crisis would be set up by the community through a committee.

Appropriate steps at forestalling the crisis would easily be taken rather than fire-brigade approach that normally leaves a negative impact on communities. Regular dialogue and discussions would eventually revive shared communities of understanding that had been denigrated by western practices across Africa. When people in a community have access to correct information, information asymmetry which usually causes misunderstanding and conflict would be minimal.

Once this institutional arrangement is established, it can be useful for information flows from bottom-up and for enlightening the grass-roots on governments' policies and programmmes as well (Akinsola 2008p:189).

6.   African Food Security Model (AFSM)

African Food Security Model (AFSM) is conceptualized as the combination of factors of production (land, labour, capital, entrepreneurship and technology) through appropriate institutional mechanisms that synergize the efforts of the key stakeholders (government, universities, industrialists and farmers) in food production (process and storage). The model has two components. The first component displays the failure of conventional food security policies in Africa as exemplified by parallel operations of the stakeholders that has resulted into food crisis. This failure calls for a paradigm shift in food security to a new institutional arrangement whereby the efforts of the stakeholders are synergized through food security mechanism (the second component). AFSM suggests that the first step is a value re-orientation. This new orientation, invariably, determines: 1. the utilization of agricultural resources 2. the development of adaptive technology and 3. the ownership of local food industries through shareholding. The outcome of the proposed new institutional arrangements is in two parts: (a) processed agricultural products, consumption of products, and exports of the products; and (b) employment generation, bonus and dividends to shareholders; and wealth creation; the overall outcome of all these is food security and poverty reduction (Akinola 2008f; p: 193-195; 2009f).

7. **African Employment Generation Model (AGEM)**

African Employment Generation Model (AGEM) is conceptualized as the combination of factors of production (land, labour, capital entrepreneurship and technology) through appropriate institutional mechanisms that synergize the efforts of the key stakeholders (governments, universities, industries and business sectors) in employment generation. AGEM sees technology development as a practice of co-creation involving social and material aspects, social and natural sciences, and societal and technological development (Akinola 2008p: 193-195).

8. **African Sustainable Environment Model (ASEM)**

African Sustainable Environment Model (ASEM) (Akinola 2008p) could be applied to reduce environmental degradation and poverty in oil communities where exploration activities are causing ecosystemic damages. Two major tools ASEM are public complaints commission for Environment (PCCE) and Environmental cost internalization (ECI). The adoption of this model in the Niger Delta will ensure stakeholders (oil companies, community members environmental related non-governmental organisations (NGOs) in the environment to jointly take decisions, monitor industrial activities and ensure that oil companies comply with Environmental Impact Assessment (EIA) standard. It is important that polluter pays legislation passed to generate revenues from oil industries. The PCCE should also ensure that part of revenue generated from oil industries should be used to provide health facilities and job opportunities for the affected communities. The process of implementing the strategy is in Six stages as discussed elsewhere (Akinola 2008q).

9.   **African Road Triology (ART)**

African Road Triology (ART) (Akinola 1998) could be applied to overcome problems that are associated with lop-sided road development. This model would assist state government and the Niger Delta Development Commission (NDDC) on road projects in the Region. The triology of roads development-survey, construction and monitoring/ maintenance (SCM) – pre-conditions durable roads and services as efficacy for master planning in providing solution to road related problems. The model establishes that road development should be placed on a tripod stand of survey, construction and monitoring/maintenance (SCM). Each Spatio-political entity-state and local government – should prepare road master plan for its geo-political area in the Niger Delta. At each level of road master plan, data relating to all roads should be generated, analyzed and projected into the future. The data, should of course, be updated in the light of some socio-economic changes that are bound to occur. The adoption of this model will, in no doubt, enable road projects to be constructed on sound footing, with ability to contain pressure of population growth in the foresee-able future (Akinola 1998; 2008q).

PROPOSAL FOR POST-AMNESTY PROGRAMME

10. African Community Initiative and Development Model (ACID)

Since it has been proved that community institutions possess requisite capabilities in mobilizing the people and resources at the grassroots, the federal government, MND, and NDDC should relate directly with these people oriented institutions. Using certain criteria such as (1) geographical location, 2) size, 3) completed projects, 4) on-going projects, and 5) future projects (in order of priority), government should identify active communities with self-help projects and pay them directly as suggested elsewhere (Akinola 2000: 186-187; 2008d). In order to solve the problems in oil communities, four things need be done (1) compensation for the affected people; (2) Reclamation or renovation of derelict land; (3) control of mining operation, and (4) allocation formula which will reflect address the needs of the affected communities has been designed and can be found elsewhere (Akinola 1999: 74). The application of this model on pilot scale and its result would go a long way in enlightening decision makers on how to resolve the Niger Delta crisis. Similarly, it would help in resolving the resource control problems. This is because it is the actual amount of money needed at the community level that the federal government would be required to pay to each community. At the same time, this strategy would help in preventing pillage and plundering by state agents in the Niger Delta (Akinola and Adesopo 2009a).

11. African Electoral Reform and Democratization (ARED)

African Electoral Reform and Democratization (ARED) could be applied to reshape, reconstruct and reconfigure democratic space to include diverse civil society, community institutions and interest groups at community and local level. ARED Model could help to connect government structures with people-oriented institutions such that elected officials (leaders) and the electorate (the led) can engage in open discussions on their problems in their tongues at community forum/assembly. The application of this model in the Niger Delta would lead to the emergence of people oriented electoral system that could constitute checks on the excessiveness of politicians. This emerging pattern of political order will invariably enable citizens and community institutions through civil society to play prominent and integral roles before, during and after elections in the Niger Delta (Akinola 2008n, p.192-193).

PROPOSAL FOR POST-AMNESTY PROGRAMME

12. African Local Economic Development Strategy (ALEDS)

Food security and poverty reduction model designed by Akinola 2006j, 2007f: 233; 2008p: 190-191 shows the relationship between the federal government, academia and industrialists. In order to eliminate all sort of exclusions in the Niger Delta, two domains of decision making – political and economic – would need to be reconstructed and reconfigured through African Local Economic Development Strategy (ALEDS). On the political level, in order to reconstruct public space, critical attention should be directed towards indigenous and endogenous institutions (ie Self-governing institutions) that the people have evolved, over the years, in coping with the problems of daily existence within their locality. Representatives of these institutions with public officials (politicians, bureaucrats and technocrats) will form community Assembly, Local Government Assembly, State Assembly and Federal Assembly. Major political decisions should be taken at Community Assembly as discussed under ALED. On economic dimension, the third tier of government should assume entrepreneurial roles so that they can generate both substantial revenues as well as employment opportunities at local level. In order to implement this model right from regional to local/community levels in the Niger Delta, there are fifteen (15) stages the model needs to pass through. The adoption of ALEDs would help in actualizing food security, employment generation, wealth creation and poverty reduction in the Niger Delta by re-orientating values.

13. **African Polycentric Privatization Model (APPM)**

African polycentric privatization model (APPM) stems from the problems that emanate from centralized political economy which breeds exclusion and marginalization of the citizenry from economic empowerment, wealth and prosperity. Except there is a deliberate public intervention through responsive policies and pragmatic steps to re-order the present centralized economic system, poverty and human misery will continue to loom large in Africa. In order to break this poverty trap in Africa, African polycentric Privatization model (APPM) is developed. APPM is conceptualized a mechanism to reverse the present centralized privatization programme that perpetuates inequality among the people of Africa. In order to avoid a situation whereby the masses of Africa would end up as the private estate of the few bourgeoisies, polycentric privatization should be adopted. APPM operates at two levels. At the first level, ownership of public enterprises should be re-distributed such that elite and bourgeoisies do not dominate the ownership arena. A new structure that would allow public and private employees to own shares is designed. At the second level, by applying part of the principles that undergird African Food Security Model, new economic enterprises should be established at various economic centres sharing ownership among the people. The outcome of this would be equitable distribution of the benefits of economic growth among citizens (Akinola 2007f: 233). APPM is designed to redistribute the outcome of economic growth by reversing the present trends using poycentric privatization mechanism. APPM mechanism is an institutional arrangement that restructure the relationship between the inputs – capital, labour, raw-materials and skills – in terms of ownership. The application of the model to the Niger Delta will increase the sense of ownership of development projects in the region by the Niger Delta citizens. What governments should do is by buying shares for the people in the industries and other economic enterprises. Through this, it is believed that the joint ownership of economic activities will restraint vandalization and economic sabotage.

PROPOSAL FOR POST-AMNESTY PROGRAMME

14. African Polycentric Security Model (APSM)

African polycentric security model APSM is conceptualized as a deliberate act of setting up new institutional arrangements, which would reflect integrative constitutional order in security of life and property (Akinola 2009a). in view of the dismal performance of the formal state structures in the delivery of services, public choice scholars have continually sought for an understanding, not only of the resilience and effectiveness of community institutions which have consistently succeeded

PROPOSAL FOR POST-AMNESTY PROGRAMME

in areas where state run institutions have failed, essentially in the provision of essential services required by the citizens. Communities are exploring pre-colonial security arrangements, resulting in huge investments in private security and community-based security arrangements. The people have exercised considerable entrepreneurial capabilities in designing institutional responses that address security of life and properly at the community level. This, invariably, calls for a paradigm shift in security system to a new institutional arrangement whereby the efforts of the stakeholders in security – politicians, bureaucrats, technocrats, scholars, and citizens – are synergized through African Polycentric Security Mechanism. African polycentric security mechanism integrates the community based security institutions (CBSLs) with the state-based organs. APSM derives inspirations and lessons from adaptation strategy of the people of Saki in Oke-Ogun, Oyo state, Nigeria. The people through collective action, have been able to transform the Oodua Peoples Congress (OPC) in their community from violent orientation to positive result such that there exists a symbiotic relationship between OPC and the local government with the community development association as the facilitator between the duo. This model suggests institutional framework that could enable stakeholders in the Niger Delta to regard themselves as participants with equal standing within security arena following the example of Saki initiatives. It is this joint action and synergy by these groups (scholars, police, public officials and representatives of community self-governing institutions, vigilantes, and investors' representatives) that would eventually determine how government policies on security matters are to be implemented. Based on the Saki Initiatives, the adoption of Polycentric Security Strategy could avail the citizens the opportunities to dialogue in community assembly and jointly take security decisions. After the institutional arrangement has been designed, operational strategy for implementation of security agenda will be fashioned out at various domains- residential, market, industrial, commercial/business, public building and roads/highway security units in the Niger Delta (Akinola 2009a: 270-271)

15. African Human Resources Development and Utilization Model (APHRDUM)

This model is designed to ensure institutional mechanisms that focus on community where both formal and informal activities converge to knowledge generation and application. For the Niger Delta people to be free from the clutch of political 'Monster', heightened human misery and poverty, human resources development that prioritizes citizens' enlightenment need to be adequately developed. This , in turn, requires that institutions that can provide effective formal and informal learning atmosphere must be established and effectively serviced. Though the need for coordination and cooperation between developers and utilizers of human resources is crucial, experience shows that the vital links between developers and utilizers are missing or not appropriately harmonized in the region. The vital links include: intellectual relevance, effective planning process and procedure, research incentives, data base and efficient communication system. Enlightened citizens pursue development agenda by drawing on their productive potentials and capabilities to achieve freedom and development. Using APHRDUM, five strategies are designed to bridge the gaps and they are 1. Africentred problem-solving and solution-seeking scholarship, 2. Africentred polycentric development planning process and procedure 3. Africentred research incentives, 4. Africentred data bank and 5. Africentred and solution-seeking designed to bridge the gaps between leaders and the Niger Delta citizens on the one hand, and between developer and utiliser of human resources on the other hand.

This section concludes that the good steps of the Federal Government of Nigeria that commenced with amnesty programme can only yield lasting dividends in term of peace and people-centred development if polycentric planning and poverty Reduction Strategy (PPPRS) is employed in the Niger Delta. In the light of this exigency, this proposal designs post-amnesty plan and programmes that can ensure economic empowerment, poverty reduction, people-centred development and peace-building in the region. The proposal develops a Niger- Delta post-amnesty Development Model (NDPADM) that derives inspirations and workability mechanisms from fifteen (15) African development models that are problem-solving and solution-seeking in several sectors of the economy in the Niger Delta.

BLOOD OIL IN THE NIGER DELTA

CHAPTER FOURTEEN

BLOOD OIL IN THE NIGER DELTA

In this chapter, effort would be focused on explaining what blood oil is all about, the blood oil business in the Niger Delta, attempts to combat blood oil by Nigerian administration and international efforts to tackle it as well as some recommendations for scaling down blood oil.

14.1. What is Blood Oil

The term "blood oil" owes its origins to the "blood diamond" campaign, which raised awareness of the problem of diamond smuggling from African war zones and its role in funding conflict. The sale of stolen oil from the Niger Delta has had the same pernicious influence on that region's conflict as diamonds did in the wars in Angola and Sierra Leone. The proceeds from oil theft are used to buy weapons and ammunition, helping to sustain the armed groups that are fighting the federal government. The armed groups are also invested in criminal enterprises such as drug trafficking. The act of stealing oil is known as "bunkering", a term originally used to describe the process of filling a tanker with oil.

The bunkering business is widespread and very profitable. One analyst, close to the former President Olusegun Obasanjo, told the BBC that it "makes £30 million (then $60 million) a day; they'd kill you, anyone, in order to protect it". Its tentacles spread beyond borders. One of the governors in the Niger Delta, the governor of Delta State, Emmanuel Uduaghan, has claimed that "anything happening in the Niger Delta today is linked to oil, and sustained by it, therefore, something like illegal bunkering has a large international dimension to it. ... All are needed to assist us to reduce the funding of the crisis which is through the illegal oil trade". However, blood oil cannot be dealt with alone: efforts against it must be accompanied by actions against the other evils that go hand-in-hand with it – corruption, illegal arms importation, and money laundering. To mitigate the dangers to Nigerians and the Nigerian government in trying to tackle this issue, it is absolutely essential for them to have proper external support.

BLOOD OIL IN THE NIGER DELTA

As an important source of high-quality oil, the 13th largest producer in the world, there are important reasons why it is in the interests of the international community – and the United States in particular – to take action. The United States, seeking to wean itself off oil imports from the Middle East, has increasingly turned to Africa as a means of enhancing its energy security. Until recently Nigeria was its fourth largest supplier, providing approximately one million barrels a day. But due in large part to supply problems caused by Niger Delta insurgency and the wholesale theft of oil, US imports from Nigeria have fallen of late. Insecurity in the Niger Delta is therefore just a problem for the United States and the wider world. At the moment, Nigeria's oil industry is producing well below capacity. Nigeria's maximum producing capacity is about 3.2 million barrels per day; however, current production is often half of that, even without OPEC quota limitations. Much of the country's production is disrupted or shut-in – the oil stays in the ground because of security threats to oil facilities and their staff of the oil that is produced, a significant proportion is lost through pipeline vandalism, acts of sabotage, and theft. A well known energy security analyst – David Goldwyn, told the Senate Foreign Relations Committee's sub-committee on African Affairs in September 2008 that if Nigeria was to produce oil at capacity, it would play a major role in helping to lower and stabilized world oil prices.

14.2. An Enabling Environment

Oil bunkering thrives in a climate of instability, conflict, and political chaos. Nigeria offers the perfect operating environment. A large, densely populated, and highly heterogeneous country of approximately 150 million people, Nigeria is a complex mixture of peoples and religions, all of whom have competing claims on an inefficient and corrupt government. There are approximately 350 ethnic groups and population is divided evenly between Christians and Muslims. Since winning its independence from Britain in 1960, Nigeria has spent more years under military regime than civilian rule. Democracy has theoretically prevailed since 1999, under the stewardship of the Peoples Democratic Party (PDP). In reality, informal patronage networks define the political system. Elections have been marred by brazen vote rigging, intimidation, and violence. Although, overall standards of governance have improved, Nigeria's economic development continues to be held back by corruption and political instability. Nigeria has traditionally been marked among the most corrupt countries in the world, according to transparency international's corruption perception index.

BLOOD OIL IN THE NIGER DELTA

The period since the restoration of democracy in 1999 has been characterized by unusually high levels of political violence centered on the Niger Delta, the heart of Nigeria's oil industry. A most cursory glance at the recent history of Niger Delta illustrates that there are many factors that help to create on environment in which oil bunkering can flourish. The Niger Delta peace and security secretariat, a group set up by civil society, the government, and the oil companies in 2005 to discuss the problems of the region, outlined a series of additional problems that have helped create an enabling environment for oil bunkering. They are:

(a)   The high number of unemployed youth in the Niger Delta;

(b)   The presence of armed ethnic militias who are familiar with the dense network of rivers that connect the region and allow easy access to unprotected oil pipelines;

(c)   The ineffective and corrupt law enforcement officials and low conviction rates for those suspected oil bunkers who are prosecuted;

(d)   The Protection or patronage offered by senior government officials and politicians who often use oil theft as a funding source for political campaigns;

(e)   The relative ease of threatening or corrupting oil industry staff to assist in bunkering;

(f)   The presence of an established international market for stolen oil, which includes West African (Sao Tome, Liberia, Senegal, Co'te d'Ivoire Gambia), Moroccan, Venezuelan, Lebanese, French, and Dutch partners;

BLOOD OIL IN THE NIGER DELTA

(g)   The overall

context of endemic corruption – traffickers "settle" as bribe local communities where the oil is tapped, "passage" communities through which the bunkering oil travels on its way to off-shore tankers, and navy officials along the route.

14.3. **The Blood Oil Business**

It should be made clear from the outset that oil bunkering by its very nature is murky, opaque business. There are many gaps, in analyst's knowledge of how the trade in blood oil operates. However, it is possible to make some general points. To begin, there are three types of illegal bunkering. The first and least significant type involves the small-scale pilfering of condensate and petroleum product destined for local market. In early 2009, the military Joint Task Force (JTF), which was brought into the Niger Delta following inter-ethnic violence during the 2003 elections, closed down a number of small local refineries where the crude was being processed for local use. This kind of bunkering is minor and conducted by local people.

A second type of illegal bunkering involves stealing crude oil either by hacking into the pipeline directly or by tapping the wellhead. This process involves removing the structure at the top (called the Christmas tree) and attaching a hose to siphon off the oil. From there, the oil is placed on small barges and taken out to sea, where it is loaded onto large ships lurking out of sight of the authorities. In return for their oil, the bunkerers receive money and weapons. The large tankers (which generally carry between 30,000 and 500,000 barrels of crude, but can carry up to two million barrels) take their cargo either to spot markets such as in Rotterdam or to refineries in other countries, such as Co'te d'Ivoire. This type of bunkering is much more significant – not just in terms of the money involved but because of what the crude oil is often exchanged for illegal weapons and drugs. There are large international syndicates involved in this operation, which also handle the money laundering for the international players.

BLOOD OIL IN THE NIGER DELTA

While Niger Delta Youth may handle the local tapping and loading, international players from Eastern Europe, Russia, Australia, Lebanon, The Netherlands, and France all play roles in financing, transporting, and laundering the money associated with blood oil. One money trial followed a path from Senegal and Co'te d'Ivoire through French banks and French credit agencies to Syria and Lebanon. It also now appears that Nigeria Lebanese (those of Lebanese descent, born or naturalized in Nigeria) are heavily involved in the business, especially those with good political connections. Similarly, many top Nigerian politicians and military officers, both serving and retired, are said by internal sources, to be actively involved in the Large-scale bunkering business.

The third type of illegal bunkering involves the excess lifting of crude oil beyond the licensed amount, using forged bills of lading, which are the documents issued by a carrier to a shipper, listing and acknowledging receipt of goods for transport and specifying terms of delivery. This type of bunkering often involves a number of oil company staff and Nigeria's state oil company, The Nigerian National Petroleum Corporation (NNPC), as well as top government officials who give the oil lifting contracts. Thus it is possible to identify the main players involved in the oil bunkering business at its various levels. At the local level, Niger Delta youth and community leaders play the leading role. As one moves up the network to the senior echelons, members of the Nigerian military, oil company, and NNPC employees, top politicians and retired military officers predominate. At an international level, the countries mentioned previously are all involved. The crews of two bunkering ships – one Filipine, another Ghanaian – were recently arrested in Nigeria and shed some light on this shadowy network.

The sheer number of players illustrates the complexity of blood oil business. It should also be noted that while Niger Delta youth often fight over bunkering turf, resulting in casualties not only to themselves but to the residents of the regions, the real benefactors are safely out of harm's way, enjoying their profits. The profits are not inconsiderable. The exact amount of oil stolen in Nigeria is unknown but it is significant. Estimates range between 30, 000 and 300,000 barrels per day. Stolen crude refers to oil taken from pipeline or flow stations, as well as extra crude added to legitimate cargos that are not accounted for. A recent study by the international centre for reconciliation (ICR) put the total value lost to the Nigerian economy from stolen crude and disrupted oil production between 2003 and 2008 at N14 trillion (approximately US $100 billion). This is a rough estimate at best because the Nigerian government does not keep statistics that distinguish between stolen crude and slut-in production, nor between losses through bunkering and losses through forged bills of lading.

Table.5: Estimate Value of Nigeria's Stolen and Shut - in Oil

Production, January 2000 – September 2008

Year	Average Price of Bonny Light per Barrel in USD	Volume of oil stolen per day (in barrels)	Value of oil stolen per annum (in USD)	Volume of Oil shot-in per day (in barrels)	Value of oil shut in per annum (in USD)	Total value of Oil Stolen or Shut-in per annum (in USD)
2000	28.49	140,000	1.5 billion	250,000	2.6 billion	4.1 billion
2001	24.50	724,171	6.5 billion	200,000	1.8 billion	8.3 billion
2002	25.15	699,763	6.5 billion	370,000	3.4 billion	9.9 billion
2003	28.76	300,000	3.2 billion	350,000	3.7 billion	6.9 billion
2004	38.27	300,000	4.2 billion	230,000	3.2 billion	6.4 billion
2005	55.67	250,000	5.1 billion	180,000	3.7 billion	8.8 billion
2006	66.84	100,000	2.4 billion	600,000	14.6 billion	17.0 billion
2007	75.14	100,000	2.7 billion	600,000	16.5 billion	19.2 billion
2008	115.81	150,000	6.3 billion	650,000	27.5 billion	33.8 billion

Source: *Coventry Cathedral, the potential for peace and reconciliation in Niger Delta (Coventry, UK: ICR, February, 2009), 159; Peace and Security Secretariat, Niger Delta Peace and Security Strategy Background papers" (unpublished paper, Port Harcourt, 2006), 25.*

The ICR report shows that although the actual volume of stolen crude went down between 2003 and September 2008, the total dollar loss to Nigeria steadily increase due to the rapid increase in the price of oil, which peaked at $147 per barrel in the summer of 2008. Figures on current levels of oil bunkering are also very difficult to come by and hard to evaluate. The picture appears to vary from company to company. While a security adviser with Chevron disclosed that theft from its pipelines in the Western Delta has practically dropped to zero, a Shell Petroleum Development Corporation staff member confirmed that bunkering was still an issue and involve individuals from host communities. Also, it was gathered that in Rivers State while bunkering by the Niger Delta youth had virtually stopped in that state, it was now being controlled by members of the Nigerian military.

14.4.   Nigerian Attempts to Tackle Blood Oil

The Nigerian government has made some efforts to control bunkering in the past. However, these efforts were usually not sustained or were executed in a half-hearted manner. The efforts included the following:

Arresting Bunkerer and Traffickers:

The Nigerian government has made several attempts to crack down on oil bunkering, dating back more than twenty years. General M. Buhari, the Military Head of State from 1983 to 1985, jailed several people for contributing to the "economic adversity of Nigeria", which perhaps was a factor in the overthrow of his government. Buhari's successor, General

Babangida and Abacha, took a more lenient approach toward bunkering. With the reintroduction of democracy in 1999, the level of bunkering increased, perhaps due to the decreased military presence in the region. Another credible theory is that bunkering increase during the run-up to election, as its profits fund attempts by political leaders to manipulate the polls. In former president Obasanjo's second term, beginning in 2003, his government began to take more serious measures to address the problem, which had began to get out of control. A number of ships involved in the trade of blood oil were seized. However, these actions seldom led to successful prosecutions. Despite of improved equipment for the Nigerian Navy, there was no marked improvement in the patrolling of the coastal waters.

BLOOD OIL IN THE NIGER DELTA

Closing Markets for Illegal Oil

The Nigerian government has urged government known to receive stolen oil to stop accepting it. It issued a warning to Co'te d'Ivoire in 2003 and offered the government in Yamoussoukro contracts for the supply of legal oil to the state owned refinery. This model might have proved effective had it been continued toward Co'te d'Ivoire and other destinations for stolen oil.

Increasing the Military Presence in the Niger Delta

The introduction of the Joint Task Force (JTF) into Warri, Delta State, following the violence surrounding the 2003 elections between the Itsekiri and Urhobo and later the Itsekiri and Ijaw ethnic groups, has not had the desired effect of controlling the blood oil business. Indeed, it has had the opposite effect of not only alienating people but of also providing military personnel with an opportunity to participate in the bunkering business, to extort money from local communities, to commit rapes, and to generally, intimidate the local populace

Introducing the Nigerian Extractive Industries Transparency Initiative

The Nigerian Extractive Industries Transparency Initiative (NEITI) was launched by the Obasanjo government and is the Nigerian version of the Extractive Industries Transparency Initiative (EITI), an international strategy launched by a coalition of non-governmental organisations (NGOs) and supported by scores of governments and international oil companies. It aims to strengthen governance by improving transparency and accountability in the extractive sector. The EITI sets a global standard for companies to publish what they pay to governments in taxes, commissions, and royalties and for governments to disclose the revenues that they receive. The Obasanjo government led the way in implementing the EITI by publishing in 2006 fully audited accounts of all the payments it received from individual companies in a five-year period. Following the inauguration of a new NEITI board in January 2008, board members resolved to cultivate a culture of transparency, accountability, due process and zero-tolerance of corruption in Nigeria's extractive Industries for the benefit of Nigerians". Unfortunately, the Yar'Adua and current Jonathan administrations have not given NEITI the necessary support to move forward. Although NEITI produced recommendations for monitoring the amount of oil stolen, it is not directly related to oil bunkering. However, it does not improve transparency in the oil industry and government, both of which would be conducive for addressing the issue of blood oil.

14.5. International Attempts to Tackle Blood Oil

The various International partners have made several attempts to help Nigeria address the issue of oil theft and violence and insecurity in the Niger Delta region. For the most part, these attempts have had limited success, perhaps due to the complexity of the problem and the actors involved.

Although it is difficult to find detailed information about earlier attempts to assist Nigeria in it efforts, recent international attempts have included the following:

Creating the Gulf of Guinea Energy Security Strategy (GGESS)

The GGESS was first conceived in a meeting attended by former president Obasanjo convened by Judith Burdin Asuri – the founder and executive director of Academic Associates Peaceworks – and Stephen Davis, then a consultant to Shell in August 2004 at which it was suggested that Nigeria should develop its own plan for ensuring security in the Niger Delta and in the large Gulf of Guinea. Obasanjo tasked the then group Managing Director (GMD) of NNPC with developing such a concept. After a lag of almost a year, the first meeting of the Gulf of Guinea Energy Security Strategy was held in Washington in the spring of 2005. GGESS grew to include the U.K and Netherlands later Norway, Switzerland, Canada, and France. NNPC was the partner organisation on the Nigerian side. After regular initial meetings, the forum has almost collapsed, with no meeting having been held since early 2008. The European partners are to reconstitute an international forum under a new minister who demonstrates more political will than the previous Nigerian focal point.

BLOOD OIL IN THE NIGER DELTA

Making Public Offers

of Military Support and Training

The British government publicly offered military support to Nigeria during late president Yar'Adua's meeting with Prime Minister Gordon Brown in July 2008, but it resulted in an uproar against "foreign military presence in the Niger Delta". It was however, discovered that, this reaction appeared to have been orchestrated by some Ijaw leaders to maintain their hold over the militants. Similar but less public offers by other countries of military training have also been rejected, with the Nigerian government requesting military equipment instead.

Developing Oil Fingerprinting Technology.

Oil fingerprinting is an analytical technique developed by chemists to identity the unique characteristics and composition of oil. Its proponents claim it is sensitive enough to identify oil emanating not only from Nigeria but also from particular fields or even specific wells. The former managing director of SPDC, Ron Van de Berg, told journalists in 2003 that certification of Nigeria's crude oil through finger printing would enable the government to block the market for stolen crude, thereby serving as a disincentive to smuggling syndicates. NNPC, the oil companies, and the UK-based University of Plymouth have been in discussion for some time about using fingerprinting to identify and certify Nigeria's crude oil going into the international market. If the origins of a cargo of oil are identified, it is possible to determine if it is legal or stolen.

Among the oil majors, opinion is divided on whether or not fingerprinting as its current stage of development is reliable enough to tie a particular cargo, or part of a cargo of oil to a precise location and therefore determine whether it is stolen. Investigation had revealed that Chevron and Total were pessimistical, they said that once the oil was mixed in a tanker, it would no longer be possible to identify Nigerian oil from other types, even though the Bonny light crude that comes from the Niger Delta is noted (and prized) for its unusually low sulphur content. By contrast, a Nigerian spokesman for ExxonMobil said that his company already possessed the technology to identify Nigerian crude, even if it was mixed with other types of oil. He further stated that his company used the technology to determine the extent of its responsibility for an oil spill as far back as 1998. A senior Shell spokesman told the Niger Delta working group in Washington D.C, in December 2008 that Shell found the Plymouth technology inadequate and was developing its own more sophisticated method, which it would give to the Nigerian government to use. As of late February 2009, the technology was still being finalized. The Nigerian government has sought international help in fingerprinting technology since at least 2005. As soon the shell technology is ready, it should be given to the Nigerian government, with strong pressure to put it to immediate use.

One problem which must be overcome is that there is currently on standard system of analysis for fingerprinting. Therefore, one company may produce fingerprints that are consistent within its own system, but another company may come up with different classifications for the same samples. The ideal would be for companies to agree on a version of analysis or at least exchange samples to create a national database.

Offering Electronic Bills of Lading:

Paper versions of bills of lading can be easily forged by either increasing or decreasing the stated volume of oil carried or changing its place of origin. As a cargo moves from place to place, the bills of lading can be altered to disguise illegal additions. Currently, most large companies (except Maersk) use manual bills of lading. However, electronic bills of lading are for better because they are virtually impossible to forge. Assistance with electronic bills of lading has been repeatedly offered by the U.S government since 2006, with no concrete response from the Nigerian government. The Liberian shipping Registry is based in the United States and monitors its flagged vessels, which carry 60-70 percent of crude into U.S. Ports. It has been suggested to NNPC and the GGESS that the registry could work on behalf of NNPC in producing electronic bills of lading. Registering vessels electronically would give real-time information about tankers and their cargo and show that the companies are not complicit in oil theft. It would eliminate the triple-dipping system, where crude is expected from Nigeria, refined, an re-imported, sometimes making several trips in and out of Nigeria before final consumption. It would also tackle the problem of "creative book-keeping" by some ship captains. Under electronic bills of lading, a small percentage would be paid to the shipping Registry, which imposes tax on all vessels flying the Nigerian flag, with most of the profit going to the Nigerian government.

BLOOD OIL IN THE NIGER DELTA

Supplying Coastal Surveillance Equipment

Equipment was supplied and installed by the U.S. government in Nigeria in 2008. The equipment uses radar sonar infrared to monitor ships in Nigerian waters, but to date there appears to have been little or no feed-back on what has been observed (although the agreement called for real-time information sharing between Nigeria and the United States). The United States also offered assistance in tracking small arms, stockpile management, and carrying out stop-and-search operations. Nevertheless, these offers have not been accepted. The Nigerian government seldom gives an outright rejection or refusal, but rather simply states that it will consider the proposal without ever giving a firm answer.

Discussing Maritime Safety and Security

Admiral Hary Ulrich of the U.S Navy visited Nigeria recently to discuss the issue of maritime security with the military and the minister of defense, but Nigerian officials were primarily interested in the provision of new equipment, such as boots and rocket launchers. When the next GGESS meeting was held in London, the Nigerian government presented to same wish list. Nigeria was also invited in 2010 to participate in the Africa Partnership stations (APS), which started with Cameroon, Ghana and Sa'o Tome', but it initially declined to take part. About eighteen months later, Nigeria's Chief of Naval staff then expressed interest in participating. The APS consist of a series of exercises in which different nationalities are trained in maritime patrols and search and rescue. Recent exercises were held in 2008 and March 2009 with Nigerian participation. Admiral Ulrich started an international network, maritime safety and security information system, which includes sixty countries in the Mediterranean, Caribbean, West Africa, and Eastern Europe. Countries in the Persian Gulf and Western Pacific will be joining soon.

BLOOD OIL IN THE NIGER DELTA

245

CHAPTER FIFTEEN

CORPORATE SOCIAL RESPONSIBILITY
AND NIGER DELTA

Corporate social responsibility (CSR) as a concept is not new. Steiner and Steiner (2006) traced the concept to the philanthropic work of business owners, John D. Rockeller and Andrew Carnegic, who offered millions of dollars to social causes. They argued that the concept of CSR was first introduced in 1954 in Howard R. Bowen's book entitled, Social Responsibilities of the Businessman; where the author stated that managers have an ethical duty to consider the wider social impacts of their decisions, and warned that the corporations that fail to encourage the broad social contract should cease to be regarded as being legitimate. There is no universally accepted single definition of corporate social responsibility CSR (Whitehouse, 2006). The concept is broad, and is split into various themes and sub-concepts, as such being incorporated by various disciplines, ranging from public policy to environmental science, which has increased the body of literature and interpretations of the concept (Carroll, 1999).

Although CSR, as stated earlier was historically thought to concern only the idea of philanthropy, it is now established that CSR has developed into an umbrella term (Whitehouse, 2006). The term now encompasses such concepts as business ethics, corporate citizenship, corporate accountability, sustainability, socially responsible investing (Ingley, 2008), and corporate community involvement (Nwankwo, Phillips, and Tracey, 2007; Seitanidi and Ryan, 2007). While Paul and Siegel (2006) define CSR as the advancement or promotion of some social good; Wood and Jones (1995) uphold that CSR is the duty for business to address social, environmental, and economic demands from stakeholders. The divergent views of the term, according to Masaka (2008) were in part due to varied social issues and societal expectations across international contexts. He however, insisted that, despite the body of interpretations of the concept, a common feature across a number of definitions that scholars have proposed on the concept of CSR is the general belief that, beyond the quest to maximize corporate profits, corporate organisations play a crucial role in solving society's problems (Masaka, 2008).

CORPORATE SOCIAL RESPONSIBILITY AND NIGER DELTA

The notion of CSR, which used to be associated with corporate philanthropy, now comprises everything from charitable contributions and social invest-ment to direct integration of the vulnerable popu-lations into a corporation's regular business prac-tice (Gutierrez and Jones, 2005). Worthy of note also is the fact that while some authors believe that CSR-based policies and programmes were initially employed by the companies in the mid-twentieth century to ward-off criticisms of their social and environment practices, others argue that lots of organizations are adopting CSR as an approach to reduce the negative social and environmental im-pacts of business as well as to maximize the posi-tive impacts of their investments, especially in de-veloping countries (Blowfield, 2005; Zadek, 2001).

Against the backdrop of various definitions of CSR,and the several activities that the concept has been used to describe, it suffices to think of the concept as an Umbrella term used to describe a variety of belief and practices. However, the ration-ale and assumptions behind the corporate social responsibility discourse can be summed up as fol-lows: (i) Corporations should think beyond making money and pay attention to social and environmen-tal issues; (ii) Corporations should behave in an eth-ical manner and demonstrate the highest level of integrity and transparency in all their operations; (iii) Corporations should be involved with the com-munity they operate in terms of enhancing social welfare and providing community support through philanthropy or other means (Banerjee, 2008).

These views capture the quintessence of CSR as conceived by the advocates of the concept, which demands that corporations should play a vital role in solving society's problems.

CORPORATE SOCIAL RESPONSIBILITY AND NIGER DELTA

According to Lepineux (2005), such supposition is based on the notion that the interest of business and the rest of society are inextricably connected; and that corporate actions are required to support the economic and social well beng of the people who constitute society. It is imperative, therefore, to have a community-based approach to CSR in which corporations play an active role in initiating social policies and community development projects (Lertzman and Vredenburg, 2005; Lund-Thomsen, 2005).

15.1 Multinational Corporations and Corporate Social Responsibility

The need for CSR is more prominent in the developing countries than in developed countries because development projects and other social infrastructure are lacking in most of these countries, and most of the time they are not provided by the government. Under these circumstances, MNCs tend to come under heightened requirements and expectations to fill these gaps (Baughn, Bodie, & McIntosh, 2007). On their own part, the MNCs acknowledge that the support given to CSR in recent years has become a constant action in corporate environment – such that companies use various communication channels like their websites, annual reports, or other promotional materials to promote the activities of CSR, in order to give Credence to the fact that the community's life and sustaining social causes are part of the significant activities that they perform.

In China, for instance, multinationals have been supportive to their host communities in several ways, with a significant part of their poverty assistance being educational aid, which itself accounts for 30 percent of all social responsibility activities, as against environmental protection and disaster relief which account for approximately 20 percent each (Samsung Economic Research Institute, 2005). The CSR activities are aimed at improving the level of education in economically underdeveloped areas, so that residents will be able to equip themselves with improved conditions of living. For example, through their CSR, Coca-cola has supported youngsters in poverty-stricken areas around China since 1993, and has maintained a strong network of schools, ranging from primary schools to universities (Samsung Economic Research Institute, 2006). The educational aid, which later incorporated youth education and vocational training are geared towards raising the educational level of the communities in view of fostering local talents and increasing potential customer base.

CORPORATE SOCIAL RESPONSIBILITY AND NIGER DELTA

Many researchers have acknowledged the importance of corporate social responsibility (CSR) for multinational corporations (MNCs) operating in developing countries, especially, the desire to attract foreign investment and jobs as a development strategy. The Global Environmental Management initiative - (GEMI, 1999) believes that developing countries recognize that MNCs investment not only provides imminent economic benefits, but also provides a crucial foundation for economic prosperity. The United Nations (1999) therefore enjoins the developing countries to achieve the necessary political and economic environment that attracts foreign direct investments (FDI), and stresses that countries lacking in FDI have economies that are heavily dependent on government regulations and controlled by inefficient state-operated monopolistic enterprises, with attendant incidences of extreme poverty, repressed human rights, and excessive environmental damage. Lodge (2006) observed that the MNCs involvement in CSR is crucial to global poverty reduction, especially in the developing countries, because poverty reduction requires systemic change, and MNCs are the world's most efficient and sustainable engines of change; offering opportunity for people who are convinced there is none, building roads and hospitals and other infrastructure.

Multinationals mostly get involved in CSR in

countries where governments are negligent of their duties of raising the living standards of the people or lack the ability to do so. In such countries, even the financial assistance provided to such countries, and meant to help the neediest citizens, most often aggravates their conditions by sustaining the corruptions of such governments that contributed to their misery, by incurring huge debts for the states. In such inefficient countries, many multinationals, apart from making the profits upon which their survival depends have often stepped into address the peoples' needs. For instance, Nestle and Unilever in India, Coca-cola in Venezuela, Intel in Costa Rica, and Land O'lakes International in Albania, just to mention but a few. Their initiatives not only provide jobs and rise in-comes, they also improve education and give individuals motivation to pursue it (Lodge, 2006).

15.2 Shell Petroleum and Corporate Social Responsibility in Niger Delta

The Niger Delta is host to a list of oil Multinationals such as SPDC, Chevron/Texaco, Exxon-Mobil, Total, Agip and their subsidiary contracting companies (Orogun, 2009). For the purpose of this section, only the CSR programmes of SPDC in the Niger Delta are examined. SPDC is the pioneer multinational oil company in the Nigerian oil industry and has remained the biggest and leading oil company in Nigeria's oil production, and 55 percent of the country's hydrocarbon reserve base. SPDC's business in Nigeria is centered in the Niger Delta, both onshore and adjoining shallow offshore areas – where it operates in oil mining lease area of around 31, 000 square kilometers. It has more than 6000 kilometers of pipelines and flow lines, 87 flow stations 8 gas plants and more than 1000 producing wells. As a corporate citizen, Shell has for a long time been committed to the development of the communities in the Niger Delta.

According to Ite (2005), Shell's initial form of community engagement dates back to the 1960s when the company supported efforts aimed at improving the livelihood of the mostly rural communities of the region. Shell has continued to demonstrate commitment to CSR by involving in programmes aimed at poverty alleviation in the Niger Delta. The company affirms that its operations strategy contributes to local development first, "through efficient and ethical standard of its business activities, in such a manner that is beneficial for both the host countries and communities, and the second is through investment that is far beyond philanthropic grants to actual technical and financial support for local development initiatives (SPDC 2004). Let us at this juncture evaluate the oil company's development interventions on poverty reduction in the Niger Delta. Here, we shall discuss the projects executed in the region by Shell under three sub divisions viz: healthcare services, educational initiatives, and youth development initiatives.

15.3

Health Care Services

In order to provide healthcare to their host communities, Shell has demonstrated concern for the health of the people of Niger Delta. This was inspired by the company's understanding that provision of qualitative healthcare cannot be the responsibility of government alone. Involvement in eradicating Malaria is one of the ways the company's corporate social responsibility is impacted in the host communities. Malaria increases the incidence of poverty as it affects the nation, community, family and individuals. The need for action on this preventable disease would no doubt reduce poverty and promote development. In achieving this, SPDC, in partnership with Africare initiated, the Africare Malaria Health Integrated Project, designed to reduce childhood and maternal mortality and morbidity in the Niger Delta though Malaria control initiative (AFRICARE/SPDC, 2009). As declared by Dr. Julius Coles, President of Africare, addressing the health needs of the people of the Niger Delta remains an under lying foundation for development of the region (Charity Wire, 2003).

Through the Malaria Health Integrated Project of SPDC, Africa has since 2003, been Implementing the 'roll back malaria' programme in 54 communities of the Niger Delta. In order to boost capacity in achieving the objective of this programme, the company provided capacity building training for some 1,074 public and private health care workers for malaria prevention and treatment, while forty seven non-government organizations (NGOs) and faith based organizations (FBOs) received grants to engage in Malaria control programmes in the communities through awareness programmes, distribution of drugs and insect treated mosquito nets (SPDC, 2004). Similarly, under the Niger Delta AIDS Response (NIDAR) projects designed by SPDC, a selected list of hospitals across five member states of the region is providing high-quality HIV/AIDS services to the patients. To achieve this, SPDC works closely with communities, national and state agencies involved in the control of AIDS, Health Ministries at both the Federal and State levels, and Family Health International (FHI) – an international NGO in the implementation of NIDAR. In partnership with FHI, SPDC completed in 2008 the $2.2 million Niger Delta HIV/AIDS response projects, with the company's share being $1.55 million. This prototype scheme trained, in its first year, 2008, more than 240 health-care providers, tested and counseled more than 4,000 people and treated more than 1,350 pregnant women to prevent mother-to-child transmission of the diseases, and enrolled 730 people for HIV/AIDS treatment (SPDC, 2009). The project was to be managed from 2009 by the state-run HIV programme. It is worthy of note that 10 more hospitals were added to the NIDAR Project in 2010, thanks to the success of the Scheme, which is geared towards providing comprehensive HIV/AIDS care, treatment and services to more people in the region.

CORPORATE SOCIAL RESPONSIBILITY AND NIGER DELTA

In order to bring healthcare closer to the people, Shell built three new community health care facilities in 2008; bringing the total number of Shell-supported healthcare facilities in the Niger Delta to 32. The facilities are staffed by more than 800 government-employed community health personnel. Some of the achievement of this gesture is that in 2008 alone the facilities treated more than 80,000 people, and helped to deliver more than 1, 800 babies; while 40, 000 people attended the health outreach programmes, which provided a range of services including health education, vaccination, eye-testing, treatment of Malaria and minor ailments, the distribution of mosquito bed nets, HIV screening and de-worming of more than 5,000 school children (Shell, 2009). In 2009 also, the facilities treated more than 265,000, helped to deliver more 2,000 babies; and reached more than 114,000 through their health outreach programmes. In 2010, SPDC and the government of Rivers state commenced the first community-based health insurance programme in Nigeria, involving the private sector, government and community, aimed at improving healthcare delivery in the communities (SPDC, 2011).

In the aspect of immunization, SPDC partners with government in the delivery of routine immunization through clinic based services in a certain group of supported health facilities as well as community based outreach activities. The company has a policy in their community health services policy to work as partners with host communities, government at all levels, local and international organisations, in order to improve the overall health of the host communities. One of the underlying principles for the company's interest in immunization has been to impact on the vulnerable members of the community and those at risk, through health activities and programmes. And to make sure the goal of immunization which ultimately is the eradication of polio is achieved, Fakunle (2010) stated that SPDC supported over 113 communities on immunization services between 2004 and 2009; and provided logistics such as boats, land transport and stipends to immunizers during national immunization days, reaching over 4.3 million children under five years of age in the communities.

CORPORATE SOCIAL RESPONSIBILITY AND NIGER DELTA

15.4 Educational initiatives

SPDC is a major contributor to social investment; and educational initiatives are a critical part of their investment. The company's educational initiative entail assisting host communities to provide sustainable and qualitative education that ultimately reaches all the people. It is the company's belief that education is a long-term investment with equally long term gestation period, and should be one of the best legacies to bequeath to individuals, groups and society. Against this background, SPDC, in partnership with NNPC, Total and Agip runs an annual scholarship programme, to support undergraduate students in Nigerian Universities. The scholarship is of two categories, namely national merit Award (NM) and Areas of Operation Merit Award (AOM). While the former is opened to the larger Nigerian Undergraduates, the later is exclusively for students from communities in which the SPDC operates. Similarly, the company runs another scholarship programme for the secondary schools across the states that constitute the Niger Delta. According to the company the secondary school scholarship scheme is to help students pay through school, as well as enhance academic achievement in the host communities.

CORPORATE SOCIAL RESPONSIBILITY AND NIGER DELTA

As most rural schools in the oil producing areas have problems attracting teachers, the company sponsors teachers in 57 community schools. Eweje (2006) noted that educational programmes of Shell in the Niger Delta comprise not only the provisions of teachers paid directly by the company and building of classrooms, but also the payment of special rates to teachers to encourage them to go and teach in remote rural areas where government are inactive. This is an expression of concern and commitment to the educational needs of their host communities.

15.5 **Youth Development Scheme**

Realizing that the youth are the hope of the future, SPDC made the reduction of unemployment among the youth a major priority for Shell Conglomerate in Nigeria, through their youth development initiatives. The Niger Delta youths, who have, over the time disrupted the oil business as an expression of their dissatisfaction, have gained real job opportunities through vocational training and job creation programmes, courtesy of Shell. The scheme, which is managed in partnership with local NGOs, has continued to offer skills acquisition training to the youths, such as in welding, sewing, auto mechanics, electrical works, computer technology, hairdressing, building, baking, soap making, plumbing and fitting. Shell stated that under the SPDC joint venture with other stakeholders, more than $2.3 million was spent in 2009 to train 306 youths in such skill areas as welding, pipefitting and carpentry, enterprise and leadership development, and conflict management. This was against the background that training can help young people acquire the skills they need in life.

Another way that SPDC has improved the lives of the youth is through their global LiveWIRE, which is a community investment programme that aims to help young people explore the option of starting their own business as a real and viable career option. In Nigeria, LiveWIRE programme, which is funded by SPDC and Shell International, seeks to add value to existing Shell's local policies and other initiatives providing support for the development of young people and their economic future. For example, he company's partnership with Nigerian telecom giant, Globacom, provided small-scale business management training, and assists people in setting up mobile phone enterprises. Since its inception, the LiveWIRE scheme has trained many Nigerian youths, including youths of the Niger Delta, giving them support to start their own small businesses. The ultimate aim of the scheme is to encourage and support youth development, specifically to help them become interested in setting up businesses and working for themselves.

CORPORATE SOCIAL RESPONSIBILITY AND NIGER DELTA

Under the LiveWIRE project, SPDC is also partnering with USAID Nigeria and the International Institute of Tropical Agriculture (IITA) in an $11.3 million project over five years to develop cassava farming. More than 3,400 farmers were trained in 2009 under this programme; 11,000 farmers received technical and business skills training; while 3,600 and 9,000 full-time and part-time jobs were created, respectively (SPDC,n.d)

In summation, it is the failure of government to provide social infrastructure and development to her citizens despite the huge revenue received from oil companies as taxes and royalties, etc that necessitated the agitations for oil multinationals to step in to fill this development gap. Corruption in government has been a major barrier to turning oil revenues into benefits for the people of Nigeria, especially the oil producing communities. For instance, between 2006 and 2010, the joint venture operated by the SPDC contributed about $31 billion to the government, while taxes and royalties to the tune of $3.8 billion was paid by Shell Nigeria Exploration and Production Company (SNEPCO) over the same period (Shell, 2011). Again, the Shell operations in Nigeria contributed over $161 million in 2010 to the Niger Delta Development Commission as required by law; while a further $71 million was invested directly by SPDC and SNEPCO towards addressing the social and economic development challenges in the Niger Delta (Shell, 2011). One should therefore, have expected some glaring development achievement from government using such enormous wealth created by Shell and other oil multinationals. However, even-though, SPDC as a company does not have all the answers or the expertise to address the development challenges in the Niger Delta, and cannot take the role of government in improving the rural areas of the region with infrastructures, it should show more active commitments to the development of their host communities from which their wealth comes from.

Federal Government and Corporative Social Responsibility

CHAPTER SIXTEEN

Federal Government and Corporative Social Responsibility in the Oil Industry: The Possibility of Corporate Social Development.

This section shall examine how well the government has been able to address its different roles and responsibilities as a means to ascertain if there is an enabling environment for CSR and therefore the possibility of corporate social development in the Niger Delta region.

16.1 Government and Its Mandating Role

Central to CSR is the need to address legal obligations (Christensen and Murphy 2004). Oil extraction by its nature tends to have a significant ecological foot print; therefore, if development efforts are to be meaningful and sustainable, they must protect, preserve, and conserve the environments upon which the livelihood of rural inhabitants depend (Idemudia 2009). This is acutely so in the Niger Delta, where 70% of the population depends on fishing and farming. Hence, governmental efforts to address its mandating responsibility vis-à-vis the oil industry are critical to community development. Fortunately, environmental laws in Nigeria are said to be in principle, comparable to those of Western Europe and North America (Hara 2001).

Indeed, a number of agencies, such as the state and federal ministries of environment and the Department of Petroleum Resources, have been established to enforce existing environmental laws. Similarly, the unanimous passage in 2004 of oil and gas bill, which stipulates the social responsibility of oil companies that operates in the country, is another important standard-setting effort by the federal government. This trend appears to have been replicated in a number of different state houses of Assembly. For example, in 2006, the Akwa Ibom State House of Assembly passed an oil bill that legislated similar provisions in the regulation of oil companies operating in the state. These bills are important because during the signing of oil prospecting agreements in the 1950s and 1980s, the guideline to protect the environment and promote good community relations were either ignored or overlooked by government and oil multinationals officials. Available anecdotal evidence thus seems to suggest that the Nigerian government might be taking its mandating responsibilities seriously.

However, the extent to which governmental attention to its mandating responsibility has reduced the costs of oil extraction for local communities and therefore supported corporate social development is at best marginal. For instance, despite widespread adoption of CSR policies by oil companies since the late 1990s, there were about 5,400 oil spills officially recorded between 2000 and 2004 alone (Onwuchekwa 2004). Indeed, local communities continue to bear the full brunt of the negative externalities associated with oil extraction, with significant ramification for their wellbeing and livelihood (see table 6). The federal government's inability to translate its mandating responsibility into effective support for corporate social development has numerous causes; we attempt only two of these causes here.

The first is the weak institutional and technical capacity of governmental regulatory agencies, such as the Department of Petroleum Resources and the federal and state ministries of environment. Due to their lack of technical and institutional capacities to effectively monitor and ensure oil industry compliance with regulatory statutes, these agencies more or less depend on oil multinationals to monitor themselves. For instance, regulatory agency officials find it difficult to gain regular access to oil industry exploration facilities in the Mangrove swamps to monitor and enforce compliance in the area. The department of petroleum Resources, and state and federal ministries of environment often lack properly equipped laboratories to undertake water and oil sample tests in the event of spills to establish the extent of environmental damage. Thus, regulatory agencies rely on oil transnationals to report on compliances and undertake sample tests. In an interview with sources in the ministry of Natural Resources and Environment in Akwa Ibom State, an engineer noted, "we have no well-equipped laboratory to test and analyze samples in the event of oil spills. As a result, the entire figures we have are based on what Exxon-Mobil chooses to release to us. That is also why the Ministry is unable to adequately arbitrate conflicting corporate-community claims in the event of oil spills or gas flaring effects".

Federal Government and Corporative Social Responsibility

This situation invariably entails a conflict of interest, since the regulated are in effect, the regulators. This has led some analysts to argue that officials oil spill records are often suspect, since many spills go unrecorded, with devastating consequences for community development. The problem of weak institutional and technical capacity is rooted in the allocation nature of the Nigerian state, where emphasis is on accumulating, distributing, and consuming rents as opposed to building the technical and institutional capacity of governmental agencies, which is perceived as diminishing instead of increasing accumulated rent.

A second factor behind government's inability to effectively support CSR relates to the nature of governmental involvement in the oil industry. Oil exploration and marketing takes place in Nigeria through complex joint venture partnership agreements in which the government holds an average of 55% equity. The Nigerian government is in effect both a direct 'stockholder' as well as a 'stakeholder' in the oil industry. Under the joint venture partnership agreements, government and foreign oil companies share the operational cost of crude oil production in proportion to their equity share, but the operational cost is fully under the control of oil companies. This arrangement means that governmental attempts to regulate the oil industry amount to government regulating itself, since it would have to bear a majority share in any additional cost that arises from governmental mandating activities. As a result, laws are often so weak they are difficult to implement, and even when such laws are enforced, fines for violations are so minimal that it is cheaper to violate than to adhere to the law. For example, Chevron noted that while compliance with the Gas Re-injection Decree that prevents gas flaring would cost the company US $56 million, it is cheaper to pay $1 million yearly in fines (Frynas 2000). It is therefore not accidental that the date for ending gas flaring in Nigeria has been shifted over several times since 1978, to the benefit of oil companies and at great cost to rural dwellers in the Niger Delta. In essence, government and oil companies find it cheaper to externalize the cost of oil extraction to local communities.

Federal Government and Corporative Social Responsibility

Local community organisations like the movement for the Survival of the Ogoni People (MOSOP) and NGOs like Environmental Rights Action have made significant efforts to resist this habit of externalizing the cost of oil extraction to local communities. While some success has been achieved, due to governmental overdependence on oil revenue so far, such efforts have been unable to bring about significant change in governmental attitude and policy. The rentier nature of the Nigerian state means that oil revenue is central to its existence. Consequently, the profit motive of oil transnationals is symbiosis with governmental interest in rent accumulation. Hence, oil TNCs are often better placed to influence government and have their interests privileged over the interests of local communities. This partly explains the relative inability of Nigeria civil society to influence how the game is played. Hence, the possibility for corporate social development in the Niger Delta is at best marginal in a context in which CSR practices are voluntary and government lacks incentive and the institutional capacity to effectively regulate oil transnational corporations (TNCs).

16.2   Government and Its Facilitating Role

The finite nature of oil and the contradictions inherent in oil extraction are well illustrated by the experiences of the people of Oloibiri in Bayelsa state. Oil was first extracted in Nigeria in 1956 in the Oloibiri community. It was once a lively town, but it is now a ghost town. Since the oil wells dried up, the people have lived a solitary and depressed life, and have nothing to show for oil extraction. If experiences like that of Oloibiri are not to be repeated and corporate social development in the Niger Delta is to become a real possibility, government needs to fulfill its interdependence responsibility to promote corporate social development via the equitable redistribution of oil wealth, the effective and efficient use of oil rent, and the unbiased reconciliation of competing and conflicting stakeholders claims. Unfortunately, the federal government has so far been unable to deliver on this responsibility.

Federal Government and Corporative Social Responsibility

First, revenue allocation and sharing are politically sensitive issues in Nigeria due to the allocation nature of the Nigerian state, as all tiers of government essentially depend on the centre for oil revenue. The problem of overdependence on oil rent within a multi-ethnic fragile state-nation, where every group seeks to maximize its gains from the national cake, allows for a politics of anxiety and the transformation of oil revenue into 'relatively assessed goods' (Idemudia and Ite 2006b). The amount of oil revenue that one state or local government gets is dependent on what other competing states and local governments receive. Hence, oil rent allocation is deeply politicized and associated with perceptions of regional and ethnic dominance that have made equitable redistribution of oil wealth difficult. For instance, prior to 2001, while the five southern oil producing state accounted for 90% of oil revenue received 19.3% of allocated oil revenue five northern non-oil producing states received 26% of allocated federal revenue (Ikporukpo 1996). This revenue allocation pattern meant that for a long time, insufficient funds were allocated to the Niger Delta. As a consequence, even though the people of the Niger Delta bore the direct cost of oil extraction, limited investment in the socio-economic development of the region has been made since independence. Hence, despite recent efforts by oil TNCs to increase their community development spending, community needs remain largely unaddressed and CSR has had limited beneficial impact (Idemudia 2009).

Second, a core characteristic of a state-nation like Nigeria is the emergence of what Ekeh (1975) refers to as the two publics. Ekeh demonstrated of the private and public realms that characteristic western societies, African Societies have two public realms with different moral linkages to private realm. The moral primordial public and the a moral civil public. The dialectical confrontation of these two publics under-pinned the proliferation of competitive communalism immediately after independence, which over time has metamorphosed into a structured, neo-patrimonial relationship that both enables corruption and makes it effective. While in principle the effective use of oil rent is another means through which the Nigerian government might facilitate corporate social development in the Niger Delta, the predomination of neo-patrimonalism-induced corruption and rentier mentality myopia has prevented the pursuit of this option. Nigeria lost an estimated US$380 billion to corruption and waste between 1960 and 1999 (Human Rights Watch 2007). The institutionalization of corruption at all levels of government and in most agencies in Nigeria effectively undermines the state's capacity to support corporate social development as revenue that could be directed toward poverty reduction is stolen. This partly explains why despite a significant increase in the allocation of oil revenue to the Niger Delta since 2000, there has been little or nothing to show for it in terms of community development (Human Rights Watch 2007). Similarly, rentier mentality myopia among government officials often means that core community development needs are neglected in favour of lofty white elephant projects. For example, instead of investing in health and education, in 2006 the Rivers state government invested in a personal private jet for the then governor.

Federal Government and Corporative Social Responsibility

Third, although oil TNCs in Niger Delta have identified conflict as a major problem confronting the implementation of CSR initiatives geared toward community development (Idemudia 2007b), instead of promoting corporate social development by encouraging stakeholder engagement and seeking peaceful means for reconciling competing and conflicting stakeholder interests, the federal government of Nigeria (FGN) has often been quick to resort to the use of force. Exemplary of this is the 1999 Odi massacre in Bayelsa state, where the Odi village was razed and over 200 people were killed under the directive of the democratic government of the time. In contrast, government provides no support to communities that decide to seek justice in the courts. This happen despite the fact that bottleneck bureaucracies, the high cost of litigation, and limited access to courts have been identifies as problems confronting this peaceful means for local communities to express their grievances against oil companies. This tendency to use force to resolve competing stakeholder claims is partly rooted in the fact that Nigeria as a state-nation face a legitimacy crisis and therefore community protest and agitation are instinctively interpreted as separatist tendencies that cannot be tolerated (Idemudia and Ite 2006b).

Federal Government and Corporative Social Responsibility

Besides, for the rentier elites, community agitation is a threat to the process of primitive accumulation within an allocative state. In addition, the minority status of the Niger Delta people in Nigeria means that their elected officials have little political leverage to influence the central state. For example, in the face of the crisis in July 2009, a House of Representatives member from the Niger Delta region moved a motion in the House of Assembly that the military assault then taking place in the region should be halted. The motion was not only defeated in the House of Assembly, but a northern 'honourable' suggested that the military action should be extended to other areas of the region and that it would be better for the population of the region to be decimated in order that oil should flow and peace should reign.

16.3   **Government and its Endorsement Role**

In theory, the Nigerian government's endorsement role provides it with an opportunity to fulfill its stakeholder accountability (see Figure 3). This role should allow the government to name and shame bad companies and reward good companies for their CSR initiatives. Unfortunately, however, the FGN does not endorse the CSR practices of oil TNCs. There are basically two possible reasons for this failure.

The first arises from the fact that both government and oil TNCs are immersed in a legitimacy crisis in the Niger Delta region (Idemudia 2007b). Each has traditionally used the failure of the other as a means of absolving itself of any wrong doing. Over the years, this blame game has become a cornerstone of Nigerian government policy in the Niger Delta. This culture of blame also extends to intergovernmental relations. While state governments accuse the federal government of failing to fulfill its responsibility to the people of the Niger Delta by increasing its developmental spending in the region, the federal government in turn blames state governments for not efficiently using the revenue they receive from the federal government. The former governor of Bayelsa state "blamed the federal government for the failure of the NDDC to meet the yearnings of the people of the region because of poor funding, and (argued) that the federal government should as a matter of urgency increase the funding of the NDDC and increase the derivation fund to 50%". In response, the secretary to the federal government recently argued that in addition to the normal revenue allocation provided to all states under section 162 (2) of the constitution, the region gets an added 13% derivation fund for crude extraction and 15% funding via the NDDC, yet the state governments have nothing to show for it. This culture of blame invariably makes any attempt by government to endorse oil TNCs' CSR efforts tilt the balance in favour of the oil TNCs and further complicate the legitimacy crisis of the Nigerian government. Governmental endorsement of CSR practices would amount to the government's conceding that it has failed, thereby opening itself to further attack. In contrast, not endorsing the CSR efforts of oil TNCs allows government to continue using the blame game to cover its own inadequacy. In essence, because governmental endorsements of oil TNCs would further damage the government's already bad reputation, highlight governmental inadequacies, and make government directly responsible for the problems in the region, endorsement is often carefully avoided.

Federal Government and Corporative Social Responsibility

The second reason government fails to endorse the CSR efforts of oil TNCs stems from the wide-spread perception that oil TNCs are socially and environmentally under-performing. There appears to be a general consensus in Nigerian society (government and host communities) that oil companies can and should do more (Idemudia 2007b). Thus, in response to an attack on Shell's Benisede flow station facilities in the Niger Delta, Dr. Cairo Ojougboh, the former chairman of the committee on Petroleum Resources in the House of Representatives, attributed the attack to Shell's irresponsibility. He argued that a careful analysis of those involved often reveals people retired or sacked by Shell, or those to whom Shell owes salaries, or the jobless in the areas where Shell operates. He concluded that "if Shell carried the people along, and gave them employment, the people would not think of involving themselves in such (attacks)". Whatever the veracity of this perception, it reinforces a view that oil TNCs are under-performing and serves to legitimize government non-endorsement of their CSR efforts.

Federal Government and Corporative Social Responsibility

16.4 Government and its Partnership Role

The Nigerian government has sought to address its stakeholder reciprocity responsibility via partnerships with oil multinationals facilitated by the enactment of the Niger Delta Development Commission Act (NDDC) of 2000. The NDDC is supposed to contribute to sustainable development of the region. The act that instituted the NDDC requires the federal government to contribute 15% of oil revenue to the commission, while the oil multinationals are expected to contribute 3% of their annual budget to the commission. In addition, member states are expected to contribute to the NDDC, 50% of the ecological fund allocated to them by the federal government. The activities of the NDDC include social infrastructure provision, health care delivery, support for agriculture, skill acquisition, and youth empowerment.

The partnership seems to have taken a strong

root in government circles for three reasons. First, there appears to be a consensus that more can be achieved by government through partnering than by working alone. A government official noted during an interview that "by partnering, the state government is able to maximize the; impact of its investment in development as well as address a wide range of community needs". Second, the pursuit of partnership appears to arise also from the dearth of resources, especially at the local government level. According to the secretary to council in Ibeno Local Government Area, Akwa Ibom state, "the local governments do not have the financial resources to provide the needed social infrastructure in the host communities due to the nature of the terrain; as such, partnership with Exxon Mobil that has the resources is a necessity". Third, there is now widespread awareness that poor coordination of development projects among government, oil companies, and the NDDC is partly responsible for community under-development due to the duplication of development projects and the inefficient use of scarce resources. As a result, partnership among these actors is seen as an opportunity for information sharing, reduction of transaction costs, and ensuring coordination (Idemudia 2009). As the governor of Delta State, Dr. Emmanuel Uduaghan puts it, "evidence had been shown that some projects which the state may have decided to undertake were sometimes on the list of NDDC and the oil companies, and this has created problems in the past, as such projects may end up being abandoned or the community will end up with just one project instead of three if the organisations involved coordinated their activities. To avoid this problem, the Delta State government has gone into partnership with the NDDC and oil companies so as to coordinate the development effort of each of them".

Federal Government and Corporative Social Responsibility

In spite of this increasing government support, partnership initiatives continue to face critical challenges. Two of these challenges are identified. The first is the Nigerian government's failure to deliver within existing partnership arrangements especially with regard to its financial commitments. A case in point is the funding of the NDDC. Even though the NDDC Act stipulates 15% contribution of the federal government to the commission, only 10-12% is always contributed, while state governments make no contribution at all. In response, the oil transnationals deduct their individual community development spending before making their 3% contribution to the commission, and in some instances, they have withheld part of their statutory contribution to the NDDC. Consequently, while by law the FGN was expected to make N318 billion in allocations to the NDDC between 2001 and 2006, it provided only N93 billion. In the same vein, while by law the oil TNCs were expected to contribute N182 billion during the same period, they allocated only N142 billion. The crucial dynamic here is that the key stakeholders (ie. Government and oil TNCs) are each attempting to pass the costs of corporate social responsibility (CSR) to the other.

As expected by those who sees CSR as good for development, CSR is in fact a domain of stakeholder contestation. Hence, the pertinent by frequently ignored question as to who should bear the cost of CSR and how this affects the possibility of corporate social development is of great importance. Government and oil TNCs are unwilling to bear the costs associated with their social responsibility, and as a consequence, CSR contribution to community development in the Niger Delta is limited. Since, the NDDC is starved of funds and therefore unable to meet its developmental goals in the region.

Federal Government and Corporative Social Responsibility

The second problem confronting the promotion of partnerships through the NDDC is political interference. The NDDC is often at the centre of political wrangling as different interest groups seek to leverage the commission, always to the detriment of its developmental goals. Nominations to the NDDC management board are more often than not, over-politicized, with significant ramifications for effective management. Similarly, mutual suspicion and acrimony among members of the joint committee of the National Assembly on the NDDC contribute to the unnecessarily long delay in passing of NDDC annual budgets. Such interference tends to destabilize and complicate the developmental efforts of the partnership responsibility. As Emmanuel Aguariavwodo, a former chief executive of the NDDC noted "the only way we (i.e. NDDC) can develop the region is to remove politics from developmental efforts. It is so important, because we face the same problems and challenges as the state governments".

16.5 Emerging Issues In Corporate Social Responsibility

There are three main issues that arose from the discussion so far. The first is that governmental support for corporate social responsibility is still limited and fragmented. Therefore, the enabling environment that would foment corporate social development in the Niger Delta is non-existent. Why is this so, and what does it means for CSR theory and practice in developing countries? Unfortunately, previous studies have been relatively silent in the face of these questions. The foregoing discussion suggests that absence of an enabling environment in Nigeria stems from structural and systemic inadequacies of the Nigeria state that are manifested in state-society relationships. While the potential benefits to be derived from partnerships between government and oil TNCs serve as an important deriver for governmental involvement in CSR, as highlighted in the literature, the analysis undertaken here identifies three constraints to the effective implementation of CSR practices in Nigeria. The first is the nature of the Nigerian state (i.e. Its state-nation status), which means the politics of anxiety often predominates so that the government is unable to either properly formulate or effectively implement a coherent CSR policy framework to support corporate social development in the Niger Delta.

Federal Government and Corporative Social Responsibility

The second is the rentier nature of the Nigerian economy, which consolidates the weak position of the Nigerian state in the global capitalist system (i.e, it is overtly dependent on oil extraction and oil revenue, but lack control over the process of oil extraction and marketing). This renders the state relatively susceptible to capture by foreign oil companies and the rentier elite, to the detriment of local communities in the Niger Delta. The third constraint is that CSR is a site of contestation informed by the logic of profitability and rent accumulation. Thus, government and oil TNCs are often willing to pass the cost of oil extraction on to local communities. This externalization of costs undermines community development via significant environmental degradation and associated health problems. These constraints to corporate social responsibility practices in the Niger Delta implicitly inhibit the possibility of corporate social development in the Delta by creating an environment in which oil companies face a high temptation to break the law, at low cost to them and with little or no associated risk for doing so (Idemudia and Ite 2006a). The implication is that since oil companies are not socially enabled to address their CSR, oil transnationals' initiatives are often fragmented, misdirected, driven by business as opposed to development logic, and based on the avoidance of core CSR issues regarded as costly to the companies, though central to community development (i.e, environmental protection).

The second emerging issue is that, in contrast to extant studies on CSR and government, which, perhaps due to their focus on developed countries, tend to suggest that government can also constrain CSR. Therefore, the issue of CSR and the possibility that it might contribute to community development is significantly different within a rentier context. The implication is that the nature of the state and the character of its economy matter for CSR and its contribution to community development. The rentier status of the Nigerian state means that government benefits more when oil companies are able to maximize profits than when they engage in costly CSR practices. Hence, support for CSR is both limited and contested. Unfortunately, the contested nature of CSR, demonstrated in the squabble over funding the NDDC and in failure of government to effectively mandate or endorse CSR, undermines the potential contribution of CSR to community development in the Niger Delta. While oil multinationals argue that community development is principally the responsibility of government, government argues that oil multinationals should be involved in ensuring the development of their host communities. Meanwhile, oil extraction continues unabated and community lands and rivers are being polluted and more people are being displaced from their traditional resources of livelihood with no alternative provided. Consequently, more households in the Niger Delta are pushed into poverty everyday. Thus, in addition to its other negative social, political, and economic consequences, rentierism also inhibits the possibility of corporate social development by constraining the ability of government to adequately support CSR and regulate oil transnationals.

Federal Government and Corporative Social Responsibility

The third emerging issue is that CSR's potential contribution to development in a country like Nigeria depends on more than whether CSR is voluntary initiative or a mandated obligation. While the call for legally binding international regulations is a necessity and a reflection of socio-political realities in developing countries, if corporate social responsibility is to contribute to development, the call for global regulation of multinationals should be situated within the broader context of efforts that seek to constrain the negative effects of capital accumulation. This means efforts to ensure corporate accountability must be undertaken in tandem with efforts to ensure state-society accountability. Regardless of whether CSR is a voluntary or mandated initiative, without a state that is accountable to its society, as in Nigeria, CSR will at best contribute only marginally to community development.

Therefore, in places like Nigeria, global regulation should be backed by social and technical capacity building of civil society (ie social forces) to enhance its relative ability to contest issues, seek accountability, and influence the state. At present, oil transnationals and rentier elites enjoy a disproportionate advantage vis-à-vis civil society in their capacity to influence and capture the state in Nigeria. In addition, civil society should broaden its strategy to engage the state by actually supporting its members in running for political office and by lobbying governmental officials. These suggestions are not without pitfalls and do not represent silver bullets, but they are among the steps that must be taken if corporate social development is to be realized in the Niger Delta.

Federal Government and Corporative Social Responsibility

Table 6:

Public Sector Roles

Mandating	"Command and control" legislation	Regulators and Inspectorates	Legal and fiscal penalties and rewards
Facilitating	Enabling legislation	Creating incentives	Capacity building
	Funding Support	Raising awareness	Stimulating Markets
Endorsing	Political Support		Publicity and praise

Partnering	Combining resources	Stakeholder engagement	Publicity and Praise Dialogue

Source: *Fox, ward, Howard (2002)*

Federal Government and Corporative Social Responsibility

Table 7:

Perceived Impact of Oil Production in Survey Village

Negative Impact of Oil Production	Villages			Total
	Emereoke1	Ikot Ebidang	Inua Eyet Ikot	₦ = 145
Damage to House roofs	41 (95%)	30 (94%)	66 (94%)	137 (94%)
Loss of Fish	40 (93%)	27(84%)	66(94%)	133(92%)
Health Problems	37(86%)	25(78%)	53(76%)	115(79%)
High Cost of Living	19(44%)	15(47%)	62(89%)	96(66%)
Low crop yield	0(0%)	26(81%)	0(0%)	26(18%)
House Vibration & Cracks	0(0%)	0(0%)	15(21%)	15(10%)

Source: *Questionnaire Survey*

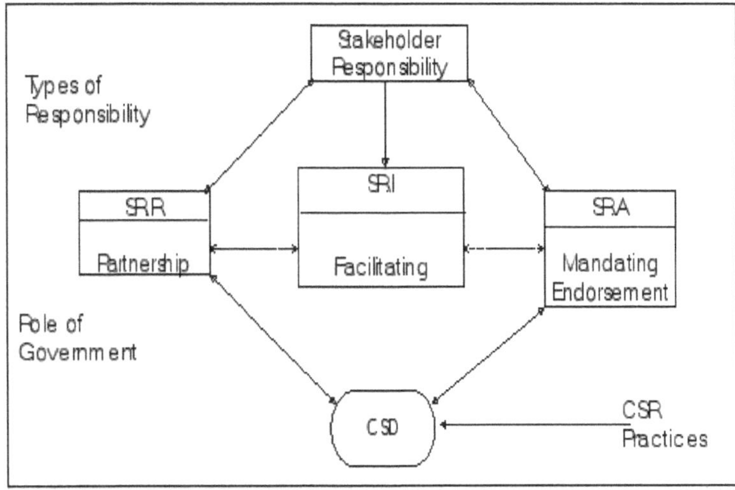

Fig.2: Conceptual Framework: government

Stakeholder Responsibility

NIGER DELTA OIL: INJUSTICE IN FOCUS

THE WAYFORWARD

CHAPTER SEVENTEEN

THE WAY FORWARD

The root causes of the Niger Delta anger, restiveness and insurgency are well known. Through the preceding chapters and pages, we were able to establish that it is an inevitable product of close to 50 years of criminal neglect; in human environmental devastation, complete exclusion of the people of the region from the benefits of their natural resources; violent and brutal onslaught on the oil-bearing communities by the Nigerian state, monumental looting of oil revenue at all levels of government; and intolerable poverty in the midst of unimaginable oil and gas wealth. All these issues have thrown up the crisis of development in the region. Hence, any attempt directed at addressing the crisis is a call for finding lasting solutions to the fundamental issues that form the bedrock of the crisis in the oil-bearing region. And one is not under any illusion to say that finding a practical solution to the problem of the Niger Delta would be easy. This is so because a part from the fact that it is a multidimensional and complex crisis, the Niger Deltans, as a result of several years of government insincerity, have become very cynical of government's intentions and policies.

However, to effectively confront the complex "Nigerian crisis located in the Niger Delta" (a la Akingemi); there is need for a pragmatic and holistic solution that is based on a sincere, visible and sustained multi-actor, multi-sectoral and intergrative interventionist mechanism in the region. As such, recommendations offer here will not only be defined on short and long term basis, it will also involve several actors: The Federal government, the Niger Delta states, the Niger Delta local government Areas, the multinational oil companies and the international community represented by countries with oil and gas interest in Nigeria, the European Union, United Nations and International nongovernmental groups such a Green Peace and Transparency International. The multi-actor character of recommendation is understandable because the crisis of the Niger Delta is not just a Nigerian problem; it is now an international issue.

THE WAY FORWARD

Government at all levels must act fast if they hope to turn back the hand of violence and insecurity associated in the region. So much lofty policies and projects have been promised to the region since this new administration came on board. Promises and good dreams or plans do not mean anything to the suffering people of the Niger Delta. The three tiers of government must as a matter of urgency fashion out an aggressive policy mechanism to address the simple and basic needs of the people of the region. The near absence of basic infrastructure such as health services and facilities, pipe-borne water, good and affordable shelter, electricity supply, road construction and maintenance, education and effective skill acquisition and empowerment programmes, must be immediately and aggressively addressed. This should be the primary policy thrust to government at all levels. And in order to sustain the process and structures, it must be done with genuine participation of the affected communities and community based organisations. It is believed that this measure will enthrone trust and confidence in the relation between the government and the people of the region. And this measure should serve as a plank for further engagement between the government and the people of the region.

Regarding the urgency of the situation in the Niger Delta region, there is a need to tinker with the philosophy, composition of the board, funding and operations of the Niger Delta Development Commission (NDDC). It is sad to that the commission has not done fairly well in the area of road construction and other infrastructures, much the same with the region's states and local governments, despite the huge financial resources allocated over the years. In its present nomenclature, the agency is too Abuja-based with members of the board and contractors federally and politically appointed. More often, the people of the region are seen as out-sider in the scheme of things. There is need for the NDDC to be made more effective and meaningful to the oil producing communities hence, the commission should be based on the bottom-to-top policy philosophy. Niger Deltans need to be put in the driving seat of any solution to their problems. Above all, the decentralization of the commission will also address the problem of undue influence of politics over development needs of the region.

THE WAY FORWARD

Below are other short and long term recommendations that need to be explored by various parties to tackle the Niger Delta problems.

17.1   What the Federal Government Should Do

☐   To promptly tackle the problem of unemployment and to engage restive youths, an enabling law should be enacted to make it mandatory for oil companies to employ bulk (at least 85 percent) of their staff at all levels from oil producing communities. Promotion of capacity building in the communities through viable educational and training programmes should also be part of the package. In the same vein, the federal government should engage seriously consider the idea of building a brand Federal Delta City (FDC), carved out of three adjoining Niger Delta states. It is believed that the proposed city which will be the hub of new petrochemical industries will constitute an employment bonanza for the teeming unemployed youths of the Niger Delta (Ekpu 2007).

☐ To limit the environmental consequences of oil exploration and exploitation, the federal government in collaboration with oil producing states and communities, should enact stringent and enforceable legislations that will ensure that multinational oil companies (MNOCs) maintain universally acceptable best standard in their operations. As part of the measure, individual company's project environmental impact assessment (EIA) studies should be made more transparent and accessible to the affected communities. In fact, they must be part of the process. This will also involve MNOCs obtaining community assent before proceeding with installation of oil production facilities, infrastructures and other developments. It is one strong believe that these measures along an effective compensation regime will go a long way to protect the culture, local economy, biodiversity and ecology of the Niger Delta region.

THE WAY FORWARD

☐ To frontally and effectively address selfish leadership and criminal looting of public funds, stringent and enforceable legal instrument should be put in place to deal with culpable public officers. The bulk of the estimated US $600 billion generated from oil production for the past 50% years, lamentably, has not impacted positively on the life of Nigerians especially the Niger Delta communities as a result of the cancerous tumor, called corruption in the Nigerian body polity. As part of its fight against corruption, it is also recommended that the government should consider a constitutional provision that will abolish criminal immunity for the president and state governors as well as encourage and empower enforcement bodies such as the Economic and Financial Crime Commission (EFCC) to prosecute cases of local and state government corruption. This is to ensure that state government allocations are spent on basic projects and services that have direct benefits on the people.

☐ The federal government should create the enabling environment that will make the people of the region real stakeholders not just spectators in the management of oil and gas resources. For example, the allocation of oil blocs should not be carried out without the genuine involvement of the community, local government and state leaders. In addition, the allocating of contracts should also have a provision that certain percentage of the proceeds for exploitation should automatically go to the affected community. The writer also agree with the proposal of professor Itse Sagay (a professor of law) that the community, local government and leaders should be represented in the supervisory and the operational arms of federal oil and gas parastatals and companies such as the Nigerian National Petroleum Company (NNPC), its supervisory department – Directorate of Petroleum Resources. (1 PR), Liquefied Natural Gas Company (LNG), Petroleum Technology Development Fund (PTDF), etc. As presently constituted, these oil and gas federal agencies are dominated by indigenes and elites of the non-oil producing majority ethnic groups. This definitely is against social justice, equity and fairness. If the Federal government is serious and sincere about addressing the agitations of the people of the Niger Delta, there must be a reversal of the current situation. Measures should be put in place to enable Niger Deltans take charge of these structures so that they could take part in making regulations to avoid pollution, determining compensations as a result of pollution; and determining how to improve production to make it pollution free (Ekpu 2007: 16). It is only by so doing that the people of the region will have a sense of belonging, identity and fulfillment.

THE WAYFORWARD

☐ In supporting the stated point, there are also proposals for a change in the joint venture agreement to enable the oil communities own shares in the oil companies. This is to offer indigenes, substantial ownership stake along the lines of what corporate majors, including Royal/Dutch, Shell, Exxon Mobil and Conoil had done in Canada and Arctic. It is believed that this step will finally put to an end the issue of vandalisation of oil infrastructure and disruption of production, as beneficiaries and real stakeholders, the communities, will make sure that oil production facilities of these companies are protected.

☐ To urgently take concrete and practical steps to diversify the Nigerian economy in order to reduced its over dependence on non-renewable oil and gas resources. Again this policy measure will strengthen the economies on non-producing states by reducing their over-reliance on federal government budgetary allocations from crude oil sales.

☐ The federal government should initiate a credible sustained dialogue on control of resources with Niger Delta Civil Society including recalcitrant militants. This will be accompanies with the following measures: one, repeal all undemocratic, exploitative and repressive laws governing the oil industry – the petroleum Act, Land Use Decree, etc. secondly, to consider the south-south proposal of 50 percent derivation of mineral resources during the National political reform conference. The increase should start from 25 percent with a marginal increase of 5 percent yearly until it gets to 50 percent; this is done so in order to avoid budgetary shock to non-oil production states and to encourage exploration and production of other mineral resources throughout Nigeria. It is expected that these policy measures will eventually lead to the denationalization of authority over oil management so that oil producing states and communities can manage the process. Thus denationalization of the oil sector is seen as the most effective means of federalizing and democratizing the nation's economic system.

THE WAYFORWARD

☐ The federal government should seek in parallel with the dialogue on resource control, an agreement with recalcitrant militants that includes a phased withdrawal of Nigerian soldiers from the region, concurrent with a weapon return amnesty programme for the remaining militants that pays them and gang members' market value for guns and enrolls in skill and job training programmes.

☐ Inaugurate a democratic constitutional reform process in which an elected assembly will work out modalities for restructuring of the Nigerian Federation in order to guarantee the ownership and control of resources by the component groups and the equality of the federating units (states).

17.2   **What the Niger Delta States should do**

• Provide effective governance and robust service delivery based on the democratic principles of equity, accountability, probity, transparency, vision, compassion and nationalism. To whom much is given much is expected. The Niger Delta states which have the largest allocations from the federation account (13 percent derivation) should be able to make their people the best sheltered, educated, clothed, fed, and empowered people in the country. The vicious cycle of poverty, anger and violent militancy in the region can only be reversed if the current governors and local government chairman are able to break away from the past eight years of ineffective, visionless, normless, unpatriotic and corruption infested governance in the region. Through accountable and responsible governance they should be able to meet the simple and basic needs of the people such as decent and affordable shelter, standard education, effective health delivery system, regular electricity supply, and road construction and maintenance. The governments of the region should focus on services and infrastructures that have direct bearing on the lives of the suffering people of the region before embarking on grandiose and lofty long term projects. In other words, emphasis now should be more on proper resource management than clamour for resource control. Such effective utilization of the 13 percent fund that will make the non-oil producing states listens to the demands of the governors of the region for increase in the derivation allocation and resource control.

THE WAY FORWARD

•   Along the same line, local government councils as the closest to the people and base on development, must be reformed and made more democratic. The grinding poverty, unemployment, and near absence of basic socio-economic infrastructure in the region has a lot to do with the non-performing local government administration in the Niger Delta. For local development there must be change of attitude and perception: local council funds should cease to be seen by political big wigs and state governors as private money to be shared among themselves and other party members. Again, to enthrone democracy at the local level, the governors of the region should stop seeing the local councils as a place fit only enough for political miscreants that carried out dirty jobs for them during elections. If government is to have any direct bearing on the lives of the people of the oil bearing communities, it is imperative to make the local government system work for the people.

•   As a matter of urgency, the state governments of the oil producing region must put mechanism in place to diversify their economic and sources of revenue. Apart from its vast hydrocarbon resources the region is endowed with other mineral resources such as glass-sand, clay marble, bitumen, bauxite, gold, iron-ore, phosphate, lead/zinc, gypsum, uranium, etc. the state governments could go into joint ventures with private investors to explore and exploit these enormous resources.

The regional governments could also go into massive investment in agriculture and agro-based industries in order to exploit its abundant agricultural endowment such as cassava, palm oil, rice, cocoa, timber, fishery and a host of other agricultural resources. It should be remembered that the Niger Delta is home to long stretches of beaches and coastal line that could be developed into a-must-visit tourist site that will generate enormous revenue for the government to the region. The Niger Delta region is more than just oil and gas. And diversification of the regional economies will not only generate money for the governments but will also generate a lot of employment opportunities for the jobless youths of the region.

THE WAY FORWARD

• State governments in the region should engage more fully with professional non-governmental organisations that demonstrate a capacity and willingness to assist communities to take responsibility for their own development.

• In their quest for resource control and denationalization of the petroleum industry, the Niger Delta states should not only build synergy among themselves, they should be tactful, calculative and diplomatic enough to build partnership and extend hands of friendship to non-oil producing states. The region should be magnanimous enough in their bargain in order to calm the fears and nerves of non-oil producing states who think that without oil revenue their governments and economics will grind to a halt. The states in the region could develop attractive loan or credit packages to assist other states in the federation to exploit natural resources in their domains. It is hoped that this will create a favourable environment for dialogue and negotiation between the Niger Delta states and non-oil producing states of the federation.

17.3   What the Transnational Oil Companies should do

(a)   Prioritize long-term interest of operating in Nigeria over short-term production goals. This also involves seeking community consent before proceeding with production related activities.

(b)   Conclude agreements to ensure prompt and commensurate payments of compensation to individuals and local communities for land use and pollution.

(c)   Develop partnership with non-governmental, community-based bodies with a demonstrated ability to provide skills training and capacity building for development projects within the affected community (Africa Report – October 2006: www.crisisgroup.org).

(d)   Only employ production techniques

and technologies that are environmentally friendly. This is to reduce the cases of oil pollution and adverse environmental consequences of oil production in the Niger Delta

17.4 What the International Community should do

(1)   Press upon the Nigerian government to abrogate its undemocratic and repressive oil related legislations such as the Petroleum Act and the Land Use Act.

(2)   Press upon the Nigerian government to initiate resource control reforms and negotiate in good faith with Niger Delta groups, and encourage MNOCs headquartered in their countries to be transparent about revenue and payments.

(3)   Provide resources for and support an independent environmental impact assessment (EIA) of the Niger Delta as well as a credible, independent judicial mechanism to adjudicate compensation claims. Steps should also be taken to ensures that compensation is distributed, transparently in a way that benefits communities rather than "benefit thieves or captors" such as greedy politicians and militants as well as traditional leaders.

(4)   A strong international mechanism should be instituted and supported by these international bodies and states against any

energy company that uses environmentally unfriendly equipment and techniques of oil and gas production.

(5)   Condition assistance to the governments upon greater transparency in federal and state budgets, particularly to energy revenue. The international community could also take more productive measure by initiating a global anti-money laundering regime that will effectively check the transnational crime of transfer of illegal or stolen money from one country to another.

(6)   Offer the good offices of a neutral country without oil interests in Nigeria to meditate between the federal government and the Niger Delta groups, an idea already accepted in principle by MEND.

The writer strongly believe that this holistic multinational and multi-actor approach will go a long to bring sustainable development, calm frail nerves and ensure peace and security to the trouble region of the Niger Delta.

BORROWING A LEAF FROM AMERICA (U.S.)

CHAPTER EIGHTEEN

BORROWING A LEAF FROM AMERICA (U.S.)

Let us examine the attitude and treatment of the United States and oil companies towards the oil-producing cities of the country vis-à-vis Nigeria. The U.S. pumps eight (8) million barrels of oil daily and the oil and gas industry provides 9.6 million jobs for Americans. By proportion, since Nigeria pumps 2.8 million barrels of oil daily, oil and gas industry should provide Nigerians with a minimum of 2.8 million jobs. But the situation on land is a far cry from the scenario in Nigeria. One of the goals of the recently formed U.S.-Nigeria Binational Commission is for the two countries to get together and resolve the Niger Delta problem. While the U.S. may be extending a brotherly hand to Nigeria, it is imperative for Nigerians to realize that they are capable of resolving the Niger Delta problem with or without U.S. resistance. All it takes is the desire to do the right thing and to standup to the oil companies who are mostly responsible for the pollution.

In April, 2011, an oil well owned by British Petroleum blew up in the Gulf of Mexico. From the day the blow up occurred to the day the well was capped, the U.S. government, the Americans, and the American media, made sure that the whole world was kept awake because of the danger it posses to the economy of the region, wild life, and the livelihood of the citizens that make their living off the gulf coast. There was so much noise, that the Obama administration was forced, by protest and persuasion to ask the culprit, BP to put aside $20 billion to settle claims of the people whose lives have been affected by the oil-spill. Thousands of citizens in and around the Gulf region were put to work to clean up the beaches. Another several hundred ships were deployed to deal with the disaster, and BP was on ;the airwave everyday apologizing to the people of the Gulf coast and the whole world.

BORROWING A LEAF FROM AMERICA (U.S.)

For 50 years, to single Oil Company that operates in the polluted lands of Niger Delta has ever apologized or created a sustained compensation plan for the people of Niger Delta. Why is Niger Delta different from the Gulf of Mexico? How can we find a permanent solution to the problem of oil spills in the Niger Delta? California has over 51,000 producing oil wells, some are pumping oil a few blocks from residential homes and business, yet one cannot recall an oil spill of major proportions that threaten the livelihood of Californians. If you spill oil in California, you have one week to clean it up face the consequences. But in the Niger Delta, the lives of most citizens that depend on farming and fishing have been destroyed for decades and yet the oil companies pass the buck back and forth between themselves and the Nigerian government.

Even the U.S government under president Obama feels compelled to do something after 30 years of ignoring the problem. While we applaud U.S government in its effort, it is hoped that the U.S. government will use the same vigor to mount pressure on the oil companies and Nigerian government to address the problems of Niger Delta just like it did for the Gulf coast. Unless a permanent solution is found to clean up all the pollution, soon or later, the people whose land are polluted will feel compelled to revolt massively.

The first objective in finding a permanent solution should be to clean up every inch of land and every drop of oil that has been spilled for the past 50 years. A thorough and planned clean up will provide immediate employment for thousands of disaffected youths that are currently taking up arms, kidnapping and disrupting the lives of the people of Niger Delta. Obviously, this will cost a lot of money, but failure to clean up and find permanent solution to the underdevelopment of the Niger Delta will be even more costly in the long run. If we start the clean up, this will immediately create thousands of jobs for the inhabitants of the Niger Delta area. Then there should need for new laws that have teeth, so to say, that will say to the oil multinationals, "if you spill, you clean, if you fail to clean, you go the jail". Legislation should be passed the levies 25% of all oil revenue from the oil transnationals which must be spent in the Niger Delta for development.

BORROWING A LEAF FROM AMERICA (U.S.)

The American tax payers have spent almost $1 trillion in the last nine years trying to contain Al Galda and other terrorists across the world, would it not make sense for us to help find a permanent solution to a potential time bomb that could disrupt our way of life the Niger Delta Struggle escalate beyond control. Amnesty programme is not all encompassing, it is seen as a palliative which may not bring permanent solution to the problem of Niger Delta. It is cheaper to clean up than to have to send American troops to sometime in the future. In fact, the American government should lead by putting pressure on both the Nigerian government and the oil companies to find a permanent solution to the backwardness and underdevelopment in the Niger Delta region. This should include a Marshal plan like loan guarantees for both cleanup and redevelopment. After all, American government did the same for Europe and Korea some years ago.

It is a known fact that the root cause of unrest in Niger Delta is poverty and exploitation. Nigerian government should formulate a policy that changes its oil and gas industry from extractive to domestication and local processing. In Nigeria, about $2billion worth of gas are burnt each year, yet the government under pressure from the oil companies has been unable to do anything about this pollution and waste of resources for the past 50 years. The reason is simple. It is not profitable for oil multinationals to recover the propane burned off daily and convert it to domestic consumption for Nigerians to use. After all, if the Nigerian government does not care about her people, why should Shell, Chevron, or Exxon Mobil care? So, there is the need to create a local processing of oil and gas, along every value claim for Nigerians to become engage and benefit thereof. Imagine how many of our people will be employed if 50 million Nigerians depend on propane to cook their food. That is a possible 50 million propane cylinders that may have to be filled monthly. This will, in itself, create an industry of cylinder makers, repairers, propane filling stations, propane tanker drivers, cylinder transportation companies and so on. No doubt, thousands of jobs will result from just one policy of ending flaring and diverting the gas to proper use domestically.

The American oil industry pumps 8 million barrels of oil daily. There are 149 refineries in the U.S.A. So, by proportion, Nigeria that pumps 2.8 million barrels of oil should have at least 52 refineries, but sad enough, the four refineries that Nigeria has are either not functioning or operating at very low capacity. It is unfortunate that oil transnationals are not interested if our refineries are working or whether they should build refineries in the country. Thus, one would suggest that another solution to the problem is to compel the oil companies to build refineries in Nigeria, thus creating jobs for the local.

BORROWING A LEAF FROM AMERICA (U.S.)

In this regard, the new Nigerian local content is a good example. The logic here is that if the people that owned the land from where the oil is pumped are not benefiting from the revenue generated, why should the people who live in distant lands benefit? Granted that these so called investors may argue that without them, there will be no revenue form the Niger Delta. While the argument may hold some water but these same companies have explorations in other parts of the world, and they make sure the owners of those lands benefit from their oil resources. Indeed, the people of the Gulf coast are not living from hand to mouth neither are the people of the North Sea. In fact, the oil companies the operate in all Western countries make sure that they invest and protect the interests of the community in which they explore. So one may ask why should it different for the people of Niger Delta?

Nigeria is the fourth largest supplier of oil to U.S.A so continuous instability in the Niger Delta will ultimately affect the fragile economy of the United States. Just like the African proverb says, "when a member of your household is eating bad insects, and you fail to warn him, sooner or later he will be so sick and will keep you up all night". If the United States, with all its influence fails to persuade the oil companies to develop the Niger Delta, the poverty and neglect will eventually give way to massive armed revolution that surpass the one witnessed during the pre-amnesty programme in the region. This may lead to total disruption of the area and possible failure of the country known as Nigeria. If the Nigerian government continues to shirk its duties by failing to compel the Oil Trans-nation Corporations operating in the Niger Delta to do the right thing, sooner or later, the elites that run and control Nigeria will no longer have a country and the people to kick around and exploit.

REFERENCES

REFERENCES

Adediran S. (2007), "Niger Delta and Security Budget", Punch, Nov. 28, 2007, P.14

Adefubi, U.A A. (1996), "Oil and the people of Niger Delta : A study of Economic, Social and Cultural Impacts of Oil Pollution, " A Research Report of Centre for development, Studies, University of Jos.

African Network for Environmental and Economic Just-ice (ANEEJ), 2004 Oil of Poverty in Niger Delta. Benin City: ANEEJ.

Agbu, Ifeatu (2011) "Nigeria: Niger Delta Ministry vs NDDC" Online source – Nigeria Masterweb Daily News.

Akinola S. R. (2003a), Resolving The Niger Delta Crisis through Polycentric Governance in Nigeria. Paper presented at a Colloquium Organized by the workshop in Political Theory and Policy Analysis, 1 December, in Indiana University, Bloomington, U.S.A.

Akinola, S. R. (1978), "Oil Prospecting, National Integration (Unity) and Sustainable Development in Nigeria", In Book of Readings on Education, Environment, and Sustainable National Development ed. Obidi, S. S. E.R.I. Afolabi, M. A. Adedibu and S. U. Kobiowu, Ibadan: Cardinal Crest Limited, pp.285-296.

Akinola, S. R. (1992), Government and The Deprived Groups: A Case of Oil Producing Region of Nigeria, Journal of Nigeria Public Administration and Management (2): 68-17.

Akinola, S. R. (2000),"Balancing The Equation of Governance at The Grassroots", In People Centred Democracy in Nigeria? The Search for Alternative Systems of Governance at The Grassroots, ed. Adebayo Adedeji and Bamildele Ayo, Ibadan: Heinemann, pp171-197.

REFERENCES
Akinola, S. R. (2004), Local Self-Governance as an Alternative to Predatory Local Government in Nigeria, International Journal of Studies in Humanities 1 (3): 47-60.

Akinola, S. R. (2007a), "Coping with Infrastructural Deprivation through Collective Action among Rural People in Nigeria", Nordic Journal of African Studies, Vol. 16(1) 2007, pp.30- 46 (online-http://www.njas.helsinki.fi)

Akinola, S. R. (2007f), Knowledge Generation, Political Actions and African Development: A Polycentric Approach, International Journal of African Renaissance Studies 2 (2): 217-238.

Akinola, S. R. (2008b) Coping with Social Deprivation through Self-Governing Institution in Oil Communities of Nigeria, Africa Today 55 (1): 89-107

Akinola, S. R. (2008d) "Polycentric Planning and Community Self-Governance as Panacea to the Niger Delta Crisis", African Journal of Development (AJD), New York University, USA.

Akinola, S. R. (2008p), "Alternative Planning Models for Development in Africa", In knowledge to Remobilise Africa (ed.), The Development Book of South African, Johannesburg: Knowledge Management Division, pp. 169-202.

Akinola, S. R. (2009a), "The Failure of Central Policing and the Resilience of Community-Based Security Institutions in Nigeria", In Adekunle Amuwo, Hippolyt A. S. Pul and Irene Omolola Adadeuoli, Civil Society, Governance and Regional Integration in Africa. Development Policy Management Forum (DPMF), Nairobi, Kenya, pp.257-274.

Akinola, S. R. (2009f), "Ensuring Food Security through Polycentric Planning and Poverty Reduction Strategy (PPPRS) in Africa.

Akinola, S. R. (2010a), "Restructuring the Public Sphere for Social Order in the Niger Delta through Polycentric Planning: What lessons for Africa?" Journal of African Asian studies, vol.9, No.1-2, Cornoll University, Ithaca, N. Y., U.S.A. pp.55-82.

REFERENCES

Akpan W. 2006, "Between Responsibility and Rhetoric: Some Consequences of CSR practices in Nigeria's oil province Development Soulthem Africa, 23, no. 2pp223-240.

Alamieyesigha, D. (2005), "The Niger Delta Crisis: Yesterday, Today and Tomorrow, "lecture delivered at the Institute of African studies, University of Ibadan, March 15.

Alapiki HE (Ed) (2001), The Nigerian Political Process, Port Harcourt: Printing and Publishing Co.

Amnesty International, 2009, Petroleum, Pollution and Poverty in the Niger Delta, London: Amnesty International Publication.

Asuni, J. B. (2009), Understanding The Armed groups in the Niger Delta, New York: Council of Foreign Relations Working Paper, September.

Azaiki S. (2003), Inequalities in Nigerian Politics, Yenagoa: Treasure Books.

Barrett L. (2008), Niger Delta: The True Story, New Africa, January 2008, pp.12-20.

Basedau M. and Lay J., (2009) Resource Curse or Rentier Peace? The Ambiguous Effects of Oil Wealth and Oil Dependence on Violent Conflict. J. Peace Res; 46 (6) 757-776.

Bassey C., Oshita O. (Eds.) 2007), Conflict Resolution, Identity Crisis and Development in Africa, Lagos: Malthouse Press Ltd.

Bisina J. (2004), Oil and Corporate Recklessness in Nigeria NigerDelta Region (www.globalpolicy.org/security/

nates/oil/2004/079reckless.htm) July 29.

Blood Trail: Repression and Resistance in Niger Delta (2002), Civil Liberties Organization, Lagos.

Boro, Isaac Jasper Adaka, (1982) The Twelve Day Revolution, Ed. Tony Tebekaemi, Benin City: Idodo Umeh Publishers.

REFERENCES

Burton, J. (1997), Violence Experienced : The Source of Conflict Violence and Crime and their Prevention, New York: Machester University Press.

Coventry Cathedral, (2009), The Potential for peace and reconciliation in The Niger Delta: Online – http:// www.coventry cathedral.org.uk/downloads/ publication

Dafinone D. (2007)   "The Niger Delta Crisis: Genesis, Exodus and Solution", The Vanguard Daily, Nov. 16th 2007, p.25.

Dawodu, Toyin (2010), "How To Solve The Niger Delta Problem online-sahara reporters.com, (retrieved 08/06/2012).

Department for International Development (2007) 'Nigeria', Country Profiles: Africa, www.dfid.gov.uk/ countries/africa/nigeria.asp (3 october 2007)

Douglas O, Okonta, l.; Kemedi D. V. and Watts M. (2004), "Oil and Militancy in the Niger Delta: Terrorist Threat or Another Colombia?" Niger Delta Economies of Violence Working Paper, No.4.

Douglas O. (1999.66), "Discussion", In T.N. Tamuno (1999), The Niger Delta Question, Port Harcourt, River-sidle Communication.

Dunning, J H. (1996) "Multinational Enterprises and the Global Economy," Addison, Wesley New Youth'

Ekpu R. (2007), "The Dilemma of Niger Delta", Newswatch. August 13th 2007, p.10-30.

European Commission (2001), Green Paper: Promoting a European Framework for Corporate Social responsibility.com (2001) 366-final, Brussels.

Eweje, G. (2006), The role of MNEs in Community development initiatives in developing countries: Corporate Social Responsibility at work in Nigeria and Southern African, Business and Society 45 (2): 93 -129.

Ezirim, G. E. (2011) "Resource Governance and Conflict in The Niger Delta: Implications for the Gulf of Guinea Region", African Journal of Political Science and Int'l Relations, vol 5(2), pp.61-71, February 2011.

REFERENCES

Fox, T. (2004), Corporate Social Responsibility and Development: In quest of an agenda, Development 47 (3): 26-36

Higgins Kate (2009) "Regional Inequality and the Niger Delta" Policy Brief No.5, World Bank Development Report.

Hopkins, M. (2006), Corporate Social Responsibility and International Development: Is Business the Solution? London: Earth-scan.

Humphreys M. (2005), Natural Resources, Conflict and Conflict Resolution: Uncovering the Mechanisms, J. Confl Resolut; 49 (4) 508-537.

Ibeanu, O. (1997), "Oil, Conflicts and Security in Rural Nigeria: Issues in Ogoni Crisis", AARS Occasional Paper

Series, Vol.1, No.2, 1997 p.10.

Idemudia, U. (2007a), Corporate Social Responsibility and Community development in the Niger Delta, Nigeria: A Critical analysis Ph.D thesis, Lancaster University, Lancaster U.K.

Idemudia, U. (2010), "Corporate Social Responsibility and Rentier Nigerian State: Rethinking the Role of Government and the possibility of corporate social development in the Niger Delta", Canadian Journal of Development Studies 30, Nos. 1-2: 131 – 153

Idemudia, U; and U. E. Ite. (2006a) Corporate –community relations in Nigeria's Oil industry: Challenges and imperatives: Corporate Social responsibility and environmental Management Journal 13 (4): 194 – 206.

Idumange, J. (2012) "Country the Gains of the Amnesty Programme". The willnigeria.com (retrieved June 7th, 2012).

Ihonvbene, Julius, "A Recipe for Perpetual Crisis: The Nigerian State and the Niger Delta" in Boiling Point p.82.

Ikejiaku, B. V. (2009), "The Relationship between Poverty, Conflict and Development", Journal of Sustainable Development, Vol. 2, No. 1, March, 2009.

REFERENCES

Ikpen, Mitaire (2012) "Niger Delta Minitry: The quest to fulfill a distant mandate", Vanguard, March 18, online source.

Ile Chinedum, Akukwe C; "Niger Delta, Nigeria: Issues, Challenges and Opportunities for Eguitable Development". Online: Nigeria World Letters & Viewpoints htm

John Idumange (2011) "The impact of Niger Delta Development Commission in the Eyes of the ordinary Niger Delta People", Online: (TNV) The Nigerian voice, 8th September 2011.

Lenin, V. I. (1984), The Three Sources and Three Component parts of Marxism, Collected Works, Moscow: Progress Publisher, 7th Edition.

Madubuike S. O; Ethnic Conflict: Social Identity and Resource Control Agitation in the Niger Delta, Dept. of Sociology, Bowen University, Iwo

Mbah G. (2008) "The Restive Youths of Niger Delta", Insider, February 11th, 2008, p.17.

National Bureau of Statistics (2005) "Poverty Profile for Nigeria", www.nigerianstat.gov.ng/connections/poverty/profile2004.pf (20th November 2007).

Niger Delta Development Commission (2005) "Annual Report 2005" Port Harcourt, www.nddcnet.com/annual -Report-2005.pdf.

Obi, C. I.(2010) "Oil Extraction, Dispossession, Resistance, and Conflict in Nigeria's Oil-Rich Niger Delta Online

OJefia I. A., "The Nigerian State and the Niger Delta Question", A Paper for The 22nd Annual Conference of The Association of Third World Studies, Americus – U.S.A., Dept. of Political Science, Delta State University, Abraka

Okaba, B. O. (2005a), Petroleum Industry and the Paradox of Rural Poverty in the Niger Delta, Benin City, Nigeria: Ethiope Publishing Corporation

REFERENCES

Okonta I, Oronto D. (2001) Where Vultures Feast: Forty Years of Shell in the Niger Delta, Ibadan: Kraft Books Limited.

Olufemi, Okofi, "Corporate social Responsibility of Multinational" Ife Psychologia, Septembers 1, 2010.

Omentte E. (2007), "The Crisis of the Niger Delta", Daily Sun, Nov. 14th, 2007, p8.

Onduku, Akpobibibo, "Environmental conflicts: The case of the Niger Delta", Online source

Osaphae E. E. (1995), "The Ogoni Uprising: Oil Politics, Minority Agitation and the Future of the Nigerian State", African Affairs, Vol.94, pp 325-344.

Oviasuyi, P. O, Uwadiae J. (2010) "The Dilemma of Niger Delta Region as Oil Producing States of Nigeria", Journal of Peace, Conflict and Development, www.peacestudiesjournal.org.uk (Retrived 23/05/2012).

Preye K. I. and David L. I. (2010), "Vexation and Militancy in the Niger Delta: The way Forward" J Hum Ecol (paper) Dept of pol. Sci, Niger Delta University and Dept. of History and Int'l Studies Unical.

Sagay, Itse (2001), "Nigeria: Federalism, the Constitution and Resource Control", Lecture Delivered at the Forth Sensitization Programme on Resource Control Organized by the Ibori Vanguard, Lagos 19 May,

Sola-I-Martin, and Subramanian, A, (2003) "Addressing the National Resource Curse: An Illustration from Nigeria", IMF Working Paper WP/03/159.

Torulagha Ps (2008), Strategic Factors and Options: Opportunity for a New Beginning, Online: www.Crisisgroup.org, (Retrieved on May 23, 2012)

Toyin Dawodu (2010) "How to Solve the Niger Delta problem", www.sahara Reports.mht

REFERENCES

Utomi, Pat, "Resource Control Fiscal Federalism and Political Stability in Nigeria", paper delivered at the Seminar on Niger Delta and Nigerian Federalism.

Wifa, B. M, (2008) "Law, Peace and Development in the Niger Delta Region" being paper delivered at the Niger Delta Development Commission (NDDC) – Nigeria Bar Association Conference, May4-7, Hotel Presidential, Port Harcourt, River state.

World Bank (1995) "Defining an Environmental Development Strategy for the Niger Delta".

World Bank: Nigeria State Finances Study, Report. No.25710 April, 2003 p.25.

www.ingramcontent.com/pod-product-compliance
Lightning Source LLC
Chambersburg PA
CBHW051433250726
48655CB00001B/37